11/00

THE HISTORY OF ARCHERY

The History of
ARCHERY

By Edmund Burke

WILLIAM MORROW AND COMPANY
New York 1957

Contents

Illustrations follow pages 32 and 128

THE HISTORY OF ARCHERY

1

The Beginnings

IN MAN'S LONG AND SOMEWHAT HESITANT CLIMB FROM THE cave to the skyscraper, he was aided considerably by the use of archery. So great is our debt to this arm that the conservative Encyclopedia Britannica ranks it as a cultural advance, comparable to the discovery of fire and the invention of the wheel. The world which we know would not exist without fire and the wheel and perhaps the same may hold true of the bow.

Most of us are familiar with archery but few of us have stopped to consider that the bow was man's first attempt at storing energy. As the arrow is drawn back, the energy is stored up in the bow itself, and at the instant of release the energy is transmitted to the arrow via the string. Prior to this innovation man had contented himself with weapons having far less efficiency. A hand-thrown weapon, like a spear or a javelin, cannot hope to compete with the arrow from a standpoint of range, power or accuracy. Even the throwing stick which early man used in conjunction with the spear is not the bow's equal. Our ancestors were poorly armed until they invented the bow and arrow.

Actually the word "invent" is a misnomer. Neither the bow nor the wheel was invented. Such processes are rather discovered, thought out or adapted from previous uses. As one school points out, the bow is not a weapon until it is used as such. The hunting bow is the same as the bow which

9

propels a drill, or even the mouth harp. It is when we fit an arrow to its string that we convert it into a weapon of offense and defense.

The date when archery came into being is the subject of debate. Most authorities feel that bows were used in Europe and Asia by the Mesolithic Period, but there is a group which holds that the bow was a product of the immediately previous age, the Upper or Late Paleolithic. The former then would date archery at about 5000 B.C., while the latter by going back one step gives it a history of ten thousand more years. It is a question which will probably never be conclusively answered, although we are inclined to agree with the scholars who place archery in the Paleolithic era. Firm support for this theory is offered by the cave paintings of Spain. These wonderful, lifelike drawings are usually equated with what is called the Aurignacian culture, which was Paleolithic—and they clearly show archers hunting. Now if the cave painters of Spain knew archery and were familiar with its uses, is it reasonable to suppose that such a much-needed weapon would have stayed on the south side of the Pyrenees for another historical era? The Mesolithic school holds that the first real evidences of archery are to be found in the shell mounds of the Ertebolle culture. The two views cannot be reconciled with any degree of ease unless perhaps we say that the Spanish cave paintings are misdated.

It must have taken many a "skull session" in many a cave before the bow was born. The need—to throw the spear farther, faster and straighter—existed, and when a problem exists man shows a remarkable ability to solve it, especially in the field of destruction. The actual facts of the case are difficult to piece together. One great legend, which occurs in several countries, is that the gift of archery was given to the people in question when they saw a porcupine throw his quills. Unfortunately the porcupine is totally incapable of discharging his barbed darts.

We can, if we like, construct an elaborate, wide-screen,

full-color story for our process, in which we have a young, muscular hero and an equally well-endowed young heroine. They are beleaguered in a cave by a saber-toothed tiger. The hero saves the maiden and the day by shooting the monster full of crude but serviceable arrows, which he has fashioned from a pile of firewood. He braids a bowstring from the heroine's long blonde locks and makes his bow from a pair of auroch's ribs which just happen to be lying about. The hero wins the maiden's hand and the chieftainship of the tribe. Man has invented archery.

In a more workaday vein and without romanticism, it seems logical that some man sat in the sun one afternoon and strung a thong between the ends of a supple stick. He amused himself by idly plucking the taut thong, listening to the twang. When he wanted to pluck the string even harder to get more noise, he substituted another stick for his fingers. This also kept him amused until on one stroke he missed and his plucker went flying. While he may not have been a scholar, he did have a great deal of native wit and when he saw his stick fly away rapidly, he put two and two together to get the answer.

This, too, is incorrect in that it is oversimplification. It may have taken years instead, but the idea is one of the most logical that can be advanced. Certainly our hero did not take his new-found weapon and go out after big game the next day.

It would be as easy to give you the year, month and week of archery's inception as to give it a birthplace. Most likely archery began in many places, just as man smelted and forged iron in different places and at different times. Historians, archeologists and anthropologists say the use of archery occurred in every part of the globe, either by diffusion or independent discovery, except in Australia and certain parts of Oceania. In the latter the explanation seems readily at hand—on the islands war was a ceremonial affair, with much hand-to-hand combat, and there was no big game which would necessitate archery's development. Why, then, don't the aborigines of Australia have the bow? Perhaps they had it once and did not develop it, because of lack of interest or need. There is a similar failure to develop a cultural tool in this hemisphere, where certain Indian tribes did develop the wheel but used it only for toys.

Today the civilized world depends on more complicated and deadly weapons for war, but there are still some backwaters of the globe where a man, to hold his place in society, must be an accomplished archer. In World War II the Commandos found the bow an ideal weapon—a shaft through the neck could silence any sentry. But our use of the bow as a means of relaxation, as a competitive weapon or as a hunting bow, is a far cry from the day when the ability to shoot with a bow was a prerequisite for survival. And the days when kingdoms rose and fell to the accompaniment of twanging bowstrings have long since passed. But it is still the same weapon and it takes the same skill to make it do what we want. If we have brought to archery the arts and sciences of today, we haven't been able to abandon the skill and practice that won the day at Agincourt.

Psychologists, who concern themselves with such matters, think our cousin the chimpanzee is gradually growing up on the evolutionary ladder. If they are right and the simians do eventually reach a stage of cultural growth where they approach our Mesolithic or Paleolithic ancestors, it will be interesting to note (if there are any of us left to do so) whether the chimpanzee "invents" the bow and arrow. We did it through necessity, and perhaps the apes will emulate, if not imitate us.

Although man created archery out of need, today we have taken to it again as one of our finest, healthiest pastimes. It is a sport which has an almost universal appeal. Young and old, men and women, rich and poor find it gives them relaxation, coordination, competition and a zest for the out-of-doors. And because it has a history almost as old as man himself, it has the added attraction of tying us to our older, simpler past, a quality much sought after in this hectic age. Fifty years ago there were only a few hundred archers in the United States. Today there are over seven and one half million—positive proof of the lure of the bow.

2

Bowmen in the Mist

To bring the archer down from the cave to comparatively recent times is a hard task. The record is full of conjecture and scattered references, consisting largely of logical suppositions with the occasional blessing of modern archeological findings. We must remember that bows and arrows and strings are perishable, and in most cases we are left to build our picture with arrowheads as the only key. Some future researchers will perhaps find our modern metal bows, but we ourselves have no such complete artifacts, and the chronicler must be forgiven if his conjectures are based more on logical deduction than on indisputable evidence.

For example, let us examine two cases which are currently in dispute. We have cited the arrowheads found in the Danish Ertebolle shell mounds as being, in the eyes of one school of archeologists, the first conclusive evidence of archery. This same school, however, will grudgingly admit that there are certain tiny flint points found in an earlier culture, the Tardenoisian, which are similar to the bird points of the American Indian. From them, can we deduce the use of the bow even earlier than the Ertebolle date? The second case is that of Folsom Man and his weapons. Some writers state that Folsom Man—from our own Southwest—had arrowheads, but other authorities are equally sure that the heads which have been found are too large to have been used on shafts and must perforce have been spearheads.

However, while it is true that such points as these are still in question, the general outlines of the development of archery are reasonably clear. Man discovered the use of archery about the time he domesticated the dog. This combination of canine helper and new weapon changed his life to a great extent. While the bow gave him stored energy and a highly efficient weapon, the dog gave him muscular cooperation, so that the hunter did not have to spend as much time afield as had his forebears. This new quasi-leisure enabled him to spend time at other pursuits, so that archery and the dog were of direct assistance in every area of cultural advance.

Although some scholars doubt that the bow and arrow arose from necessity, it is certain that its spread was rapid. Says A. L. Kroeber in his work *Anthropology:* "The basic innovations that came up in the Mesolithic era were the first domestication of any animal, the dog; pottery; and perhaps the bow. All three of these became far more important later than they were at the time; their appearance in the Mesolithic seems to have been adventitious rather than in a response to a felt need."

Man lived to hunt and he hunted to live. As the centuries passed, he experimented with his weapons, changing the design and the materials until he achieved—for the time and the place—the ultimate weapon. Time and place are important, for the bow is by its very nature subject to the fullest development in those geographic areas which are best suited to its employment, such as steppes or savannahs. The archery of Central Asia was the best in the world because of this fact. Conversely, in other areas the use of archery is geographically and developmentally confined, as was the case with the Mayas of Central America, who never really developed archery but clung instead to the more primitive and less effective spear thrower.

The early hunters lived in caves or in crude shelters of little or no permanence. Communication between families and clans was nearly always the limit of experience. The sept or family moved only when it became necessary due to the migration of game or to some drastic change of climate during the great ages of glaciation. The only law was strength—strength to guard, strength to attack, to defend, to lead and to feed. Prior to the inception of the bow, the physically strongest had been the leaders, but with archery and the dog it became possible for the average man to fill the needs of primitive law equally well. The bow served as a leveler and became the hunter's most prized possession. When a man died, only those things which were truly his were buried with him; and recently discovered burial grounds in the Lake Baikal region show that the bow was always included in the grave.

Other changes were taking place and altering man's future. As a hunter, he had to have game. Sometimes it was plentiful, but at other times the situation was different. Herds moved about, some species died out entirely, and sometimes whole seasons went by when meat was scarce. In sheer desperation, the hunter and his family experimented with other foodstuffs. The value of seeds began to be appreciated and the first grain was sown. Man found that with cereals stored away it was not so necessary to venture out of his cave or hut when the snow lay deep and packs of wolves howled in the forest. Man began to move to spots where grain grew more plentifully and easily. He learned to smoke his excess meat so that it did not rot in a few days. Then, too, some more advanced individuals learned that meat could be kept indefinitely simply by leaving it on the hoof. Meat could be kept in a pen, and when one wanted a roast he had only to step into the pen with a big club or a sharp spear.

These foresighted ones had troubles, nonetheless. If they had been fortunate enough to find a good plot of land along some river bottom, there were sure to be other groups who hadn't been so lucky, who did not have a crop of cereal to tide them over the winter, who had not learned to smoke or sun-cure meat, or who were too lazy to go through all the trouble of penning livestock. The "haves" found the bow and the spear and the rock were just as effective in holding off a human enemy as they had been against the more primitive animals. And the "have-nots" came to just the same conclusions, though for different ends. If a deer had fallen before the flight of an arrow, so would some primitive husbandman.

So to protect himself, his goods and his chattel, the farmer and his clan began to build walls to guard against enemies, animal and human. The town had begun.

Other hunters chose to go after the game. Certainly one of the great sources of the world's people was and is Central Asia—a magnificent land, full of infinite variations of climate and geography, with towering snow-capped mountains; barren, hellish deserts; fertile oases; and the never-ending grass-covered steppes. And it was here the bow reached its highest point of development and spread outward with the people.

Here, too, man gained the second of his great animal companions. The earliest inhabitants of the area had lived, to a great extent, on the huge herds of mammoths, but when the mammoth retreated to the far north and finally perished, new sources of food had to be found. The hunters found they needed all their skill to keep from starving, for the animals were swifter of foot than their human attackers. The hunters were especially attracted to one animal—the tarpan. Shaggy, ugly, with a straggly beard and a long tail that swept the ground, the tarpan was the fleetest animal the hunters had ever seen. It was only a matter of applied logic to capture the tarpan and ride him, so that the hunter became as swift as his quarry, so that the bow and arrow could do their deadly work within a reasonable distance. With time the tarpan grew bigger—his legs lengthened, his beard disappeared, his body grew shorter and rounder. The hunter had a horse.

With the horse the hunter acquired not only speed but almost total mobility. Having no house, no land and no ties,
it was simple for him to mount and ride to some new spot
where the game was thicker, where the grass was greener,
and where there were no towns to interfere with his way of
life. Small groups of riders surged across the vastnesses of
land and where they found things to their liking, settled, if
but for a time. Since their culture was a fleeting, self-contained
thing, we have no real record of where they went or where
they stayed. Primarily they were interested in meat for
themselves and pasturage for their horse herds. Only when
they made contact with sedentary populations do we have
any record of their movement.

Here and there, however, there were isolated pockets of
horsemen who proved the exception to the rule and stayed.
Or sometimes they were pockets that resulted from a move by
Central Asiatic hunters before the coming of the horse. A
tribe of hunters, having trekked across half a continent,
might find themselves in a position where it was impractical
either to go forward or to turn back along the path they had
followed. One such enclave started out from mid-Asia in
pursuit of the retreating mammoths and came to rest along
the top of the Scandinavian Peninsula. Here, to what is today
northern Sweden, Norway and Finland, came tribes of short
dark men. In the snows and forests of this new land the
hunters stopped, their way forward blocked by the sea,
the path back crowded with other forward-pressing tribes.
There they stayed, keeping the old tradition of shamanism,
clinging to the old tongue, following the old way of hunting
with the bow. Centuries later, another great migratory wave
rumbled up from the south and met these Finno-Ugric
settlers. The Teutonic tribes, coming north from Central
Europe, met them and drove them north into the most barren
sections. But the Teutons, who ultimately became the Vikings
of Scandinavia, adopted the bow from their northern neighbors. As far as we can tell, the Teutons were not archers al-

though they may have had bows. When they stopped along the fjords of Norway and Sweden they took a page from the Lapps and Finns and became ardent followers of archery. Later, when they went "a-Viking," they took with them the bow and spread it as a weapon of offense and defense wherever they established their colonies.

Because archery and its tools are dependent on environment, it is interesting to examine what amounts to a modern-day Neolithic archer and his equipment. The culture of the Bushman of South Africa has proven a happy hunting ground for the anthropologist, since it represents a survival of Stone Age peoples up to the present day.

The bow of the Bushman is extremely light, with a pull seldom exceeding thirty pounds. The wood used for the bow varies, some being made from certain canes. All over the continent of Africa, cane has been used for bows from time immemorial. The arrows are composed of two parts: the shaft proper, which is usually tough reed, and the head, which is made of fire-hardened hardwood and which is over three inches long. The head is easily detachable, and when the arrow strikes game, the shaft drops off so that the hunter can retrieve and rehead it. Often the Bushman's only costume is a band of cloth or bark wrapped around his forehead, which is used to carry spare arrowheads.

Like many American Indians, the Bushman does not depend on the strength of his bow to bring down the game, but rather on his ability as a tracker and a stalker. One report from an early Afrikaans source says that two Bushmen once ran down an antelope in a matter of fourteen hours. Too, the Bushman, like other African primitives, has another ace as far as archery is concerned—the use of poison on his arrowheads. The exact formula is not recorded but in general it consists of the venom sacs of poisonous snakes, the roots and leaves of poisonous plants and trees and the bodies of certain poisonous caterpillars. The whole is boiled down to form a waxlike jelly which is used to smear the tips. With this equip-

ment the Bushman was superb as a hunter, completely nomadic and self-sufficient. Only the coming of the white
man and the raids of the Kaffirs served to destroy his Stone
Age life, driving him into the vastnesses of the Kalahari
Desert.

Unlike the Bushman, the people of Central Asia developed
complex bows at a very early date. In the first period,
around Lake Baikal, the bows and strings found in burial
sites were simple self bows. The term "self" is applied to
any bow made of a single material, like the English longbow, which was made of yew wood. The term "composite"
describes any bow utilizing more than one material in its
construction.

Thus in the second period, called Serovo by the Russians,
the composite bow had made its appearance. This bow had
a wooden body, but the back was reinforced with strips of
sinew, bound to the body. Also the limbs were beginning to
take the classic recurved form. We can safely assume that
two factors entered into the revisions which culminated in
the fully recurved, composite Asiatic bow. One would be
the comparative scarcity of suitable bow woods in areas of
steppe land. To compensate for this lack the bowyer would
experiment until he arrived at the sinew backing to give his
bow the needed power. Secondly, since these people were
horse nomads, the recurved form, which is easier to make in
a composite bow, was much better suited to their needs,
with increased cast and maneuverability while the rider is
in motion. With his horse and his modified bow the nomad
became the terror of the known world—and continued
so until after the empire of Timur Leng, or Tamerlane.
Riders on horseback, shooting their arrows from the recurved
bow while at full gallop, drinking the blood of their
mounts and eating their flesh, were quite capable of meeting
and defeating any army.

Another interesting fact comes to light in these Serovo
burials. Women have been found with the recurved bow

in the grave. Does this indicate a race of warrior women, who fought side by side with their men? And if so, does it account for the later legends, current during the time of Herodotus, about the Amazons? Certainly the burials would indicate that the women used the bows, else why bury them with the weapons?

One later burial site, discovered in Siberia, casts another odd light on archery. Here the warrior is buried with his wife and child. Such interments are not rare, but in this case the widow and child were killed by being shot full of arrows.

All over the world during this time, tribes were moving in waves. A season of drought searing the grass, and some tribe must move—into the territory of another tribe. Pressures built up and were transmitted over great distances. Wars came, kings rose and fell, other tribes moved, more pressures were created. No matter the area, the primary weapon of the moving tribes was the bow. The negroid cultures of Southern India died under the attack of archer Aryans, who poured into the rich maw of the subcontinent, crossing the mountains from their steppe homes. The Shepherd Kings of Egypt, the Hyksos, were chariot drivers, but their first weapon was the bow. The pre-Homeric tribes of Greece and the Islands went down before bowmen from the north and east. Each time pressures of economy and space had created waves of people which rippled or roared out from the cradle places, changing the whole complex of civilization at any given period.

But there was beginning to be a pattern of empires, which survived or absorbed the waves that lapped about their borders. A certain amount of stability was hardening the racial molds. And with this hardening and stability the archer begins to come closer to us, to a point where we can examine him and his weapons with more certainty.

3

The Old Kingdoms

A ROLL CALL OF THE MIGHTY KINGDOMS OF THE PAST SEEMS TO draw back the curtain of time, to give us a glimpse of things as they were. Possibly the oldest of them was China, which went through some twenty dynasties in the course of her history and who may, for all we know, be starting another today. China is like a gigantic sponge, absorbing people, customs and culture alike, molding master and vassal into the Sino-pattern. During one period when her borders were being constantly breached by nomad bowmen, China lost sixty million people in a ten-year period. Yet such was the fertility and fruitfulness of the land and the people that within another twenty years the loss in lives had been completely replaced.

The Chinese, as we know them today, came to their land from somewhere in the west—again the pressures and the moves, driving individuals, tribes and hordes. Who lived in China before the Chinese? A hard question and one to which you will not find the answer, except perhaps for one clue. In the islands of Japan are the remnants of a race called the Ainu, a people classified as Caucasoid. They were the tribes displaced when the Japanese came to the islands from the west. Perhaps they had also lived on the mainland in even earlier times.

Archery in China goes back to one of the first thoroughly investigated periods—the Shang Kingdom, which is dated from 1766 B.C. to 1122 B.C. In the capitol of the kingdom, An Yang, archeologists have uncovered the royal palace and immediately adjacent royal workshops, which included those set aside for the arrowsmiths. Other remains from the Shang indicate that war was conducted from chariots, a common custom in all of those old kingdoms. In addition to the driver, each of the Shang chariots carried a lancer and an archer. Thus each chariot combined offensive power, the bow—and defensive strength, the lance. Cavalry, as such, was introduced into China at a later date, during the Ch'in period. Between the Shang and Ch'in lies an interval of wars and movements which is vague, although one race stands out as a special enemy of the Chinese. This was the Wu, a nation of seafarers who went out from their coastal homes in huge war canoes, wearing high feather headdresses and taking the heads of their victims as war trophies. They were not essentially archers but one series of engravings from the era shows the Wu using a primitive bow.

China continued to use archery right down to the present. Her history is interwoven with wars which featured the use of archers, both foot and horse. Across the narrow Sea of Japan, the island people used the bow from their first settlement. During Samurai times the bow was one of the warrior's principal weapons, and today the Japanese still practice a highly stylized form of the sport, linking it metaphysically with Zen Buddhism.

Across the continent and toward the south lie the Tigris and Euphrates rivers. Here in the fertility of their floodlands, another great civilization had its day. Almost as old as the Chinese culture, the Assyrian and Babylonian kingdoms are far more familiar to us by virtue of their Biblical connections. Here, over five thousand years ago, the rich land was exploited by many tribes, tribes whose histories told no tales of coming, but simply existing there since the very beginning of time.

Here Assur and Babylon, Ur of the Chaldees and Nineveh

were the centers around which hundreds of other towns and cities grew. The people knew and used advanced methods of irrigation, reclaiming both arid and swampy lands to produce bumper crops for centuries. Here Akkadians and Sumerians, Amorites and Elamites, Hittites and Aramaeans, Subarians and Mitannians came and went, ruling and being ruled. Here Sargon and Sennacherib, Tiglath-pileser and Hammurabi, Shalmaneser and Nebuchadnezzar ruled as kings and emperors, as astrologers dictated to the lives of commoner and noble alike.

Because the land was rich and fertile, it was fought over many times. The people grew used to war and created standing armies besides the usual levies of city and town militia. The bow was used, but to all intents and purposes was an arm for the nobility. Sculpture from the period shows extremely short bows with out-of-proportion arrows. When the bow was unstrung, the two limbs formed almost a forty-five degree angle and when it was drawn the limbs came round in almost full circle.

The extreme length of the arrows used in these kingdoms remained a mystery for centuries, until an archer in Pennsylvania duplicated the bow and proved that it was possible to shoot a four-foot shaft from a five-foot bow. Unlike the later Egyptians, who used only the bow from the chariot, the Hittites imitated the Chinese in the use of a three-man chariot force—again, driver, archer and lancer.

Records from the period note that the bow and arrows were important enough to be mentioned in trial proceedings. The bow had achieved legal status.

The Hittites also used the bow in their magic, or primitive medicine. There is extant a treatise which covers the cure for loss of sexual strength. The formula, which may have been a primitive attempt to combat homosexuality, worked equally well for men or women. Since we are concerned primarily with bowmen, the male treatment is given here.

The victim was clad in black garments from head to foot, including plugs of black wool inserted in the ears. After a period of incantation by the officiating medicine man or woman, the clothing was removed, the earplugs were withdrawn and the nude patient was handed a spindle and made to pass through a ceremonial gate. When he emerged from the gate, the spindle was taken from his hand, and he was given instead a strung war bow. The practitioner then spoke in ritual form, "Behold, I have taken away from you womanhood and have given you back manhood. You have cast away the manners of women and have taken up the manners of men."

Although, as we have said, the bow in war was essentially a weapon of the nobility, there are scattered references to bodies of archers, known as "Sutu." The Sutu was used for light, swift attack, acting as a hit-and-run weapon against the enemy's defensive positions. Basically, however, the common foot soldier was armed with sword, lance and dagger while the rich rode into battle in chariots, pulling their grotesquely short bows. Cavalry played little part in the battles until around 1600 B.C., and then only as a branch of invading forces. From 3000 B.C. to 539 B.C., when the last of the Babylonian-Assyrian complex of empires fell to Cyrus of Persia, this west Asian area was the greatest center of civilization on the Asiatic continent.

Nearby was Egypt, a land lying along the Mother Nile, bound inextricably to her. There, in Paleolithic times, a simple hunting people had lived where the desert came sweeping down to the swamps and marshes of the Nile shore. Quietly they lived and quietly they passed into oblivion, for there is no real mark to show the break between these simple hunters and the equally simple pastoralists who followed them in the Neolithic Age. The men of the New Stone Age tended their flocks along the banks of the great river, where annual floods insured some of the richest soil in the world. And like all men who settle down, they followed the routine of village and town building. Houses of pressed mud and baked mud sprang up along the river.

As hunters, these original Egyptians were bowmen. And as herdsmen and agriculturalists, they depended on their bows to drive off the lions of the desert and to defend themselves against the raids of nomadic tribesmen from the vast Libyan Desert or from Abyssinia.

Another factor in the history of Egypt was coming in from the north. Groups of tall, long-headed Asiatics were following the course of the river from the Delta to the edge of the Sudan. Warlike and cultured, they subdued the natives and acted as their rulers. Probably they came from what is now Syria, some authorities crediting them with being the progenitors of early Babylonia, as well as "dynastic Egypt." A third factor came into the picture with the continuing raids of Lybian tribes. These were as warlike as the "dynasts" but lacked their cultural background. Physically they were similar to today's Nilotic negro stock—tall, thin, roundheaded and barbarous.

Civilization along the fertile Nile spread at such a rapid pace and made such great advances that scholars are at a loss to account for its impetus. Even predynastic Egypt was incredibly cultured. They possessed a working calendar in the year 4000 B.C.

In another field, too, there was progress. As early as the Sixth Dynasty (circa 2600 B.C.) there was regular conscription for the Egyptian army. Each young man of good health had to join a levy raised either in his town or his farm area. The recruits served for varying periods of time, depending largely on the need for their services.

This army was the result of the union between Upper and Lower Egypt at the start of the First Dynasty. Chronology shows this union occurring around 3400 B.C., with eight kings in the dynasty.

Egypt did not become a militaristic nation until the period

of the New Kingdom. Before that, under the leadership of the "dynasts" the nation was busy consolidating its own lands and settling the affairs of the dynasties which rose and fell like so many waves of the sea.

Suddenly, stark disaster struck Egypt, in the form of the Shepherd Kings, the Hyksos, who hit into the fertile Nile country from across the grim Sinai Peninsula. Driving like the wind, these nomads took over the country, as one chronicler reported, without having to strike a blow, and when they could no longer hold the Egyptians in thrall, they raced eastward and vanished, as suddenly and completely as they had come. The puzzle of the Hyksos is still an enigma for historians and Egyptologists. The records of the time are fragmentary and Egypt's neighbors seem to have left her alone during the rule of the nomads, sending in no observers. For two dynasties, the fifteenth and the sixteenth, Egypt was in complete subjugation.

The Hyksos left one gift for the Egyptians, in the form of the horse. Prior to their coming there had been no horses along the Nile. The Nile people used the horse along the sandy areas surrounding their fields and in time became the best charioteers in the world, but strangely enough there was never an Egyptian cavalry. Later in the course of Egyptian empire there were cavalry units, but without exception the horsemen were mercenaries from outland.

The system of conscription continued and we find a record of Amenhotep III holding as one of his titles, "Director of Recruiting." Under his direct supervision, the young men of the nation were accepted or rejected for military service. Armed with bow and arrows, shield and lance, the draftees underwent a program of drill, gymnastics and heavy manual labor. When the drill masters felt their charges were becoming lax, they put the soldiers at work dragging monuments, statues and blocks of stone.

The bows issued to the men were weak by our standards, and by the standards of other primitive armies. One reason for this lay in the fact that the troops were very lightly armored, due to the extreme heat of the country. Since it wasn't necessary to penetrate thick armor, the bowyers of the Nile continued to construct light bows, of a composite construction. In line with other stories which have come down to us about legendary bows, Amenhotep III (1400 B.C.) is supposed to have had a bow with such a stiff pull that no other man in the two kingdoms could string it, let alone loose an arrow from it.

At the end of the Hyksos reign the Egyptian commoner had become more warlike, had developed military abilities and in consequence the Empire began a period of expansion, utilizing these new-found talents. While the foot soldiery was still composed of spearmen and archers, something new had been added here, as well. Although the quiver was known in the Old Kingdom, it did not come into general use until after the expulsion of the Hyksos. Thus, where previously the Egyptian archer had gone into battle with his extra shafts in his hand, he now carried them in a quiver. With added fire power at his command, the Egyptian bowman was able to fire in volley. Even before this time the Egyptian bowmen were feared by their foes, and now their military reputation became such that it lasted well into classical times.

Egyptian arrowheads were peculiar to the Nile. Up to the Thirteenth Dynasty they were made of flint, although metal had long been in use. Prudently the Egyptians worked on the assumption that an arrowhead was expendable and metal was far too valuable to waste when flint would do the job. This conservatism was quite common in various cultures. The peculiarity of the heads lay in their shape. Instead of forming the traditional triangle, the Nilotic head came to a flat surface, like the biting edge of a front tooth. We have no way of knowing what specific purpose this design served, but it continued to be used until the introduction of mercenary troops into the Egyptian army.

For everyday hunting even flint was avoided, the points

being simply hardened tips on the shafts—completely self-arrows. It was only in big hunts, when the game was gazelle or perhaps the lordly lion that the shafts were actually tipped. Then the archer stood upright on a swaying chariot, while the horses raced to bring the hunter abreast of his game. It required top-notch skill on the part of both the charioteer and the archer to make this form of sport a success. Often enough, when they hunted lion, the tables would be turned and the hunter dragged from the chariot, or the galloping horses dragged down. Like the Assyrians and Babylonians, many of the Egyptian war archers were similarly chariot-borne, and whether they hunted men or animals, the quiver was always slung alongside the chariot, where the archer could easily grasp his shafts.

Amenhotep III was perhaps the most distinguished of the royal archers of Egypt. It is recorded that he was fond of hunting wild cattle, which sometimes came down into the Delta. The royal gamekeepers were under strict orders to drive the cattle into a huge pen and notify the Pharaoh. On one occasion Amenhotep, hearing that a large group had been sighted, left his palace and sailed all night to be at the hunting grounds by dawn. Entering his chariot, he was driven into the enclosure and in one day's shooting brought down fifty-six wild cattle. Later he commemorated the day's hunt with a series of scarabs. He is also noted for issuing a series of scarabs every ten years, showing the number of lions he had killed. One text reads: "Statement of lions which his majesty brought down with his own arrows from the year one to the year ten: fierce lions, 102." One of the earlier pharaohs, Thutmose III, is recorded to have organized a huge elephant hunt from chariots, while resting between campaigns. At war with the Mitanni in the Near East, Thutmose ordered his troops to round up the North Syrian herd of elephants, which at that time numbered some 120 animals. Going in for a close shot, Thutmose was threatened by the trunk of an enraged bull but was saved by one of his generals, Amenemhab. Seeing the danger which threatened the Pharaoh, the warrior prince recklessly ordered his chariot between and then with a mighty blow of his sword he severed the trunk of the elephant.

When the New Empire was firmly established, the kings of Egypt set off on a round of wars and conquests which set the nation up as one of the strongest of its era. Egyptian arms ranged north along the Mediterranean littoral and south into the mountains of Abyssinia. Their Lybian neighbors continued to be troublesome, and the kings, thinking to fight fire with fire, hired large bodies of the tribesmen as mercenaries. This, however, did not serve its prime purpose, for we read of the dessert raiders acting in concert with their allies, the "Sea People." The chronicles go on to list these seafarers as the Teresh, Ekwash, Sherden, Shekelesh and Lukku, names we today equate with the Tyrrheni or Etruscans, Achaeans, Sardinians, Sicilians and Lycians. Later combinations of tribes fighting as allies with the Lybians included the Cretan ancestors of the Philistines and what are tentatively identified as the Danaï or Greeks.

The Philistines were often a thorn in the side of the New Empire. Living side by side with the Semites, they had taken on the culture of their neighbors; originally they were not of Semitic stock, but came from Asia Minor and were European in appearance. Opinion differs as to their route before coming to the Egyptian borders. One school holds they came directly down the coast, fighting as they moved. Another feels they came to Asia Minor after having sojourned with cousins on the island of Crete. The latter premise is supported in part by the fact that the Philistines were excellent archers and Crete was for centuries the home of archers famed throughout the world. This was a Crete which came after the peak glories of Minoan civilization. Between the sea kings of Knossos and the monarchs of Egypt there had for centuries been a thriving interchange. Pottery, tablets, figurines and hundreds of other artifacts prove the point for century after century. Suddenly the exchange ceased, apparently coincidentally with a vast upheaval of people in that end of the sea. The lords of Knossos never regained their power and the island of Crete broke down into dozens of petty, bickering monarchies. Gradually a Cretan social system evolved under which there were but two classes—free men and serfs. The serfs were slaves—owned by individuals or by the state. Like Sparta, all the free men were citizens and warriors. Each youth joined a "herd" when he reached the age of seventeen. Prior to that he had learned to read and write. At seventeen he put these childish things aside and became an apprentice warrior. He spent his whole life in perfecting military skills, with particular emphasis on archery, for Apollo, the Archer God, was the patron of Crete. For relaxation the young warrior was allowed to marry, but he was not permitted to live with his wife until he had become a full-fledged man at the age of twenty-five. Soon Crete was overrun with warriors and they sold themselves to the highest bidder. They fought in every major war around the Mediterranean and most of the minor ones. When generals and kings wanted archers they sent to Crete for the cream of the crop.

With the end of the sea kings' power, the seat of authority in that end of the Mediterranean passed north to Greece, to the land of Apollo and Zeus, of Hera and Athena.

Greece and her isles had had a race of prehistoric peoples, known as the Pelasgians. Their name is taken to mean either "sea-farers" or "shepherds." Their last survivors were supposed to exist on Crete. Possibly they were short, dark and long-headed. Even their language is lost, but the British author and historian Robert Graves in a series of works has endeavored to show that they were followers of a primitive, tripartite goddess. Since such a worship was prevalent in the area, his supposition cannot be far from wrong, but aside from this we have almost no concrete evidence about these pre-Hellenic Greeks.

Driving the Pelasgians from their homeland, came a race known as the Ionians. A few years ago it was customary to teach that they and the two successive waves of invaders who overcame Greece were barbarians from the north and the east—Macedonia and Thrace. Today that theory has lost many of its adherents, new schools having sprung up to claim that the new tribes came from Crete, Italy, Asia Minor, Turkey or the shores of the Black Sea. Since it hasn't been completely disproven that the old "men from the north" idea is wrong, it is still a reasonable solution to the problem.

After the Ionians came the Achaeans. It is of the Achaeans that Homer wrote, although he actually lived hundreds of years after the time of Achaean domination. From his scanty references to their physical characteristics, these were taller men than either the Pelasgians or the Ionians, with fair hair and gray or blue eyes. During the peak of Achaean Greece there was a very close interchange with Crete. With the fall of Knossos, the culture which had previously been called Minoan spread to the Achaean-dominated Greek archipelago and mainland, where it was identified with Mycenae. Today we speak of the total cultural pattern, both Minoan and Mycenaean, as Aegean.

Both the Achaeans and Ionians were, in their prime, races of feudal overlords, actively enforcing their will on the native populations. They built towns which centered around a few strong fortress-homes and held the common people in a state bordering on serfdom. Every bit of archeological activity to date has pointed this out and it followed then that the last of the great waves, the Dorian, should follow the same pattern. Even had their predecessors not been warriors, the Dorians would have had to rule feudally in order to maintain their mastery. In the beginning the Dorians had the distinct advantage of possessing iron, which the Bronze Age Ionians and Achaeans did not. But before peace was finally established among the three races, iron had spread, with

Top: Archery Wrist Guard, made of coiled reed. Egyptian. Dated circa 2700 B.C. Bronze Arrowheads from the same period.

Right: Oldest preserved bows known. Made of acacia wood and excavated at Beni Hassan. Dated circa 2000 B.C.

Bottom: One of the earliest known arrowheads. Excavated in North Africa and tentatively dated circa 10,000 B.C., from the Alterian culture. Flint, chipped with precision and comparable in penetration and flight accuracy to many modern heads.

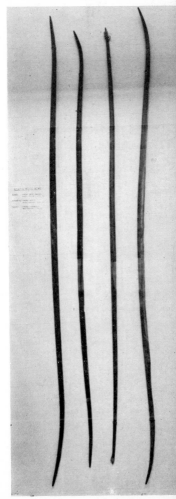

Top: Assyrian Horse Archer at full draw. Note extreme curve of bow limbs and extreme anchor point, i.e., well behind ear. *Bottom:* Assyrian Horse Archer riding with unstrung bow.

Assyrian hunter shooting from a pit. Apparently nobleman, since youth is employed to pass him arrows. May have been shooting at birds. Again, note extreme draw.

Archers besieging a city. Note that with each archer, there is a second man holding a wicker shield to protect the bowman.

The Lion Hunt of King Assur-Bani-Pal, central figure showing the king about to loose an arrow. Behind him, spearmen drive off a wounded lion, not shown.

Warriors (archers) in procession, carrying unstrung bows.

Norman rock drawing of an archer. Scratched into the wall of Colchester Castle, Colchester, Essex, it is probably the earliest representation of an archer in England.

French Medieval Print showing woman archer.

Line drawings by William E. Tucker.

Upper left:
Eskimo

Upper right:
African

Bottom:
Negrito

war, throughout the land and the islands. The classical Hellene was a polyglot, melded in fire and war.

Archery was well known to the pre-Dorian Greeks. According to Pliny, the Greeks attributed the art to either Scythes, the son of Jupiter (Zeus), or to Perses, son of Perseus. In a later period, we shall see how interesting either of these names is, from a standpoint of peoples who later bulk large in Greek history.

In Aegean Greece, it was customary to raise large flocks of geese, but not for their meat. Rather the birds served as the source of good feathers for fletching the arrows of the warriors.

Hercules, or Herakles, the Greek demigod, was famed as an archer and most of his statues show him equipped with bow and arrows.

There is one story which stresses his ability as an archer. Hercules was returning home with his wife Deianira when they came to the river Evenus. Nessus, the centaur, was the ferryman, but his craft was so small that he could only carry one passenger on a trip. Accordingly he crossed first with Deianira, leaving Hercules on the bank. When Nessus and the girl reached the other side, he dragged her off, intent on ravaging her. Hercules, outraged, fitted an arrow to his bowstring and sent one shaft speeding across the Evenus to fell the centaur. Then in his rage he leaped into the river and swam across. The swim was pointless, since Nessus had died almost instantly, but before the end he persuaded Deianira to dip her cloak in his blood, saying that it would hold the love of anyone. Years later when Hercules was looking with sheep's eyes at another woman, she thought of the centaur's words and made Hercules wear the cloak.

The hero was poisoned from the contact and staggered out into the air. In agony he made his way to a mountaintop where he built his own funeral pyre. By that time he was too sick to light the pyre and a passing shepherd, Poeas, came up to watch the hero's death throes. Hercules pleaded with the shepherd to put a torch to the pyre but Poeas would not do so without a bribe. Then Hercules gave him his bow and his quiver of arrows. Poeas fired the pyre and Hercules went the way of a hero, while Poeas returned home with the arms.

The legends of the era are numerous but we owe our greatest debt to Homer, for his re-creation of the Achaeans and their lives. His two chronicles of the Trojan War have made that conflict the most celebrated of all time. We must remember that Homer was writing centuries after the events actually occurred. And in the best bardic tradition he was passing the tale along with embroideries. If in his telling he ignores economics and stresses personalities, we can only take pleasure in the tales. If the outcome was not in the hands of the warriors but, rather, determined by Olympian whim, we enjoy it nonetheless.

The seduction and abduction of Helen bring about the teller's desired effect—the gathering of kings and princes, the altercations which threaten to throw Olympus into permanent discord. So the kings and their allies gathered on the shore before Priam's city and laid siege to it. If, as Homer would have us believe, the attack was ten years in length, we can only think that the battle was intermittent. There could only be a certain number of the Achaean warriors spared from the tasks of home rule. It seems probable that the chieftains took turns in besieging the walls of the city, while their off-duty colleagues went home to keep peace in their territories.

Another theory is that the first nine years were pure poetic license and that the siege actually was of only one year's duration.

But we see the war through other eyes, the eyes of Blind Homer, who parades before us an array of heroes—brave, vain, valiant, jealous, courageous, petty, bickering, close-fisted, generous. In other words, much like the soldiers in any army. We see Patroclus clad in the armor of invincible Achilles, parading around the walls of Ilium. Achilles himself lies in his tent, sulking over some small offense. Patroclus walks with a strut to imitate Achilles perfectly, the Achaeans are losing heart and from the battlements the Trojans make mock of them. Along the walls the Trojans run, keeping pace with the armored figure. Then to the battlements comes Hector, Prince of Troy and the bravest of the warriors within the walls. He watches the parading man and then calls for a bow. Swiftly he fits a shaft and, drawing to his eye, lets drive at the strutter down below. Patroclus falls and a shout of horror rises from the Greek camp.

Word of his death is brought to the tent of Achilles and he leaves his couch and goes forth to make his peace with Agamemnon, war leader of the Greeks. Clad in new armor, he mounts his chariot and drives in fury round and round the walls of Troy until Hector comes forth to give him battle. Then ensues the fight between the warrior champions of the two forces, ending in the death of the Trojan. From the walls, Priam, father of Hector, has seen the slaughter and he comes out on the plain to beg of Achilles that the body of Hector be returned. His request is granted and Achilles returns to the siege.

Again, within the walls of Troy, the hero Pandarus comes to the walls. Says Homer, "Forthwith he unsheathed his polished bow of horn of the wild ibex." Vowing a gift of one hundred lambs to Apollo, the Lord of Archery, if his arrow strike Menelaus, "he drew his bow, holding in the same grasp the arrow-nock and the bowstring of ox's sinew, and stretched back the bowstring as far as his breast, and the iron arrowhead as far as the bow, and when he had drawn the great bow into a circle [Note: similarity to Assyrian bows] the bow twanged and the string hummed aloud and the sharp arrow sped forth, keen to wing its way into the press . . ." The arrow strikes Menelaus, but Athena intervenes, stopping some of its force—". . . on the clasped belt it struck and down through the rich belt and through the curious corselet, on through the metal-studded apron which he wore to guard his flesh against darts, and this it was defended him best, but this too did the arrow pierce, grazing his outermost flesh, and straightway did the dark blood pour from his wound . . ."

A Greek soothsayer has predicted that the walls of Troy will never fall unless the bow and arrows of the dead hero Hercules are in the Greek encampment. Poeas, long dead, had bequeathed the weapons to his son Philoctetes, who was one of the warriors who had started for the siege ten years before. But on his way he was bitten by a serpent and had been at home recovering for the past ten years. Diomedes and Odysseus are sent by Agamemnon to fetch the sick warrior, and on their return, a Greek physician heals Philoctetes of his festering wound. Homer also records that all of Philoctetes' oarsmen were expert archers.

Achilles has in the meantime been slain by an arrow from the bow of Paris, the brother of Hector, and the Achaeans are once more desolate, having lost their battle champion. But with the arrival of the historic bow and arrows, they take heart again, and Philoctetes, going into the fray, sees Paris on the walls and, using the arrows of Hercules, kills the second son of Priam. Shortly thereafter the Greeks build their dummy horse and Ilium falls to the victorious besiegers.

But for sheer force, the greatest archery scene in the Homeric myths comes when Odysseus, King of Ithaca, returns to his home after twenty years of wandering. Here he finds his wife Penelope under a different kind of siege. Fifty suitors demand that she choose one of them for spouse. Unrecognized, Odysseus confides in his son Telemachus and the two plot the downfall of the suitors.

One evening Telemachus announces that his mother has finally decided to take her pick. The man among them who can string and shoot her husband's war bow shall have her hand. During the following day, Odysseus, Telemachus and two faithful servants take all the arms and armor down from the walls of the banqueting hall. That evening the suitors try to string and shoot the bow, which has lain in its case for twenty years.

(To insert a technical note: Homer speaks of two bows, that of Pandarus and that of Odysseus. He does not describe the latter, but the former he says is made from the matched horns of a goat killed by Pandarus. Let us assume that both bows were of a similar design and construction. Unfortunately it would be impossible to make a workable bow from the horns of a goat. In the first place, goat horns are hollow. If the horn and its filling were used, the bow would be so stiff that even Hercules would be unable to pull it. If the horn itself—that is, the outer shell—were used it would still be too stiff for practical use. It is far better to assume the Homeric bows to have been deeply recurved composites, with horn of some sort serving as the back of the bow while the belly would have been of sinew. The sinew was probably covered or gilded, so that Homer in describing the finished weapon would assume that the whole was made of horn—two limbs of perfect match being set together by a bronze handle. The theory of a composite is borne out by the fact that the bow was kept in a case for the twenty years, and that Odysseus did not take the bow with him on the sea voyage to Troy. The primitive glues in use during that period would have made it necessary to take special precautions in handling such a bow, with sea air one of the worst enemies.)

Telemachus goes down the courtyard from the tables and sets up twelve war axes in a row, their open throats in line. At the far end he places a target. The suitors, between flagons of wine are trying to string the great bow, without success. Odysseus is in the hall, dressed in beggar's rags, and the suitors mock him and scoff at Telemachus for permitting him to enter the palace. One of the suitors throws a bone at

Odysseus, but the king never gives away his masquerade. Finally a servant is sent for warm oil and soft wool to try to soften the bow.

When this proves unsuccessful the leaders of the group decide to abandon the project. Odysseus signals for the bow and it is brought to him, while the suitors howl in derision. The king fondles the bow amid asides, "Look, the fool fancies he knows bows," "Maybe he saw a bow once before," "Ho, Telemachus, what insult is this to give your father's bow to a beggarman?" The test arrow is at Odysseus' feet and he sits on a stool, caressing the bow. "Then as easily as a skillful musician stretches a new string on his harp, fastening the sheepgut over the pegs at each end, so without an effort Odysseus strung the great bow . . . He took one sharp arrow which lay out on the table before him; the others were still in the quiver, but those present were soon to feel them. This he laid on the bridge of the bow and drew back the string and notches together; still sitting upon his chair as he was, he took aim and let fly. He did not miss: right through the tops of all the axes went the shaft and clean to the target at the other end.

". . . Now Odysseus stript off his rags and leapt upon the great doorstone, holding the bow and the quiver full of arrows. He spread the arrows before his feet and called aloud to the suitors:

" 'So the game is over. And now for another mark, which no man has ever hit. I will see if Apollo will hear my prayer and let me strike it.'

"Then he shot straight at Antinous, the leader of the men who plagued his wife. He was holding a large golden goblet in both hands, and about to lift it for a drink . . . the arrow struck him in the throat and the point ran through the soft neck. He sank to the other side and in an instant a thick jet of blood spurted from his mouth, so lately oped for wine . . . Then Eurymachos spoke out:

" 'My friends, this man, this Ithacan Odysseus, come back, will not hold his hands, he thinks he is invincible . . .'

"With this he drew a good sharp blade from his side and leapt at Odysseus with a yell; but on that instant Odysseus let fly an arrow and struck him in the chest by the nipple. The sharp point pierced his liver; down fell the sword from his hand, he folded up and fell sprawling on the table, food and wine spilling to the floor whilst Eurymachos beat his forehead on the ground in agony, his feet kicked out and a mist came over his eyes . . .

"As long as the arrows lasted Odysseus went on bringing down the defilers of his household one after another. But when the arrows were at an end and he could shoot no more, he placed the bow against the lintel post and left it standing. . . ."

So the king came home to Ithaca to wreak his vengeance with his bow and the sharp, swift, silent arrows. A fitting note to close the Homeric age and the story of the long-dead kingdoms.

4

Greece—Persia—and the Heirs

AFTER HOMER, OR MORE PROPERLY, AFTER HOMER'S HEROES, came the development of the Greek city-states. Here flourished the cream of Greek culture, the philosophy, the architecture, the sculpture, the literature, in fact all that we call "the glory that was Greece." This was the Greece of Demosthenes and Pericles, of Euripedes and Solon, of Plato and Aristotle. Here too lived Lycurgus, the Spartan.

Lycurgus, the Lawgiver, is of interest in the history of archery only in an indirect way. But because he bulks so large in military history it is worth while to examine the state which he bequeathed to the world, at least according to Greek chroniclers. Sparta was the most militaristic of the city-states and operated under a code of laws which were handed down by Lycurgus. Some authorities feel the man never actually existed; others claim he was one of Sparta's early regents. In any case Sparta gives us a picture of a militant communism, working at a very early date. One historian has described Sparta as a "happy brotherhood of warriors," and it seems in fact to have been just that.

At or before the age of six weeks, every male child of free birth was brought before a council of the elders. At this time, the men decided whether the child was physically fit to become part of the state. Should their decision be in the negative, the baby was taken outside the walls and exposed on the rocky hillside, either to die of starvation or as the prey of animals. Those chosen as fit were returned to their families for the next seven years.

For that brief span the child was part of a family unit, but a militant one nonetheless, since his father was a soldier. At seven the boy became a charge of the state.

He lived from then on in barracks, drilled, marched and studied the then fragmentary military history and learned to excel in every form of tough physical sport. Food was simple, tobacco unknown and alcohol used sparingly, if at all. A "Spartan life" was just that—austere, militant, regimented and dedicated.

At twenty, after having undergone thirteen years of this training, the Spartan boy enrolled in one of the "dining messes" and was subject to draft call. Since the entire nation was under arms, it is easy to see why Sparta was always ready to take to the field of battle. At thirty, the Spartan, if he had fulfilled his military and social duties, was awarded the rights of a full citizen. At sixty, he was finally rid of his military duty and could relax in the happy thought of sons and grandsons replacing him while he sat in the sun.

Although the Spartan boys and men early learned the use of the bow, their invincibility lay in the phalanx of the hoplites or foot soldiers. This was a solid hedgehog of men, its forefront bristling with long spears, which advanced at a steady pace to meet the enemy. At times the phalanx was eight men deep and the width of the line adjusted to terrain or objective. Heavily armored (the hoplite carried over seventy pounds of helmet, shield and body armor; on the march each hoplite had one or two body servants to carry the armor), the phalanx, until the evolution of military tactics, was a nearly unstoppable human tank. When phalanx met phalanx, as was often the case, particularly during the Peloponnesian War, it was a matter of discipline and courage as the two masses met head on. There was no attempt at turning a flank, no wheeling attack, only march and countermarch with the inevitable mass contact.

In Sparta, since all free men were active soldiers, the other work necessary for the actual support of the state was done by helots, who were, to all intents and purposes, slaves. But in the other parts of Greece, where the militaristic caste did not predominate, the farmer and the shopkeeper formed the ranks of the phalanx. When the call to arms sounded, each man pulled down his armor and went off to defend the city. Standing armies came into being quite well along in the history of the city-states, and Plato, a firm supporter of archery, mentions a standing body of archers, a thousand strong, who manned the city of Athens. Aeschylus records the presence in Athens of an archer-police force from the year 480 B.C. on. These men were Scutai or Scyths, imported and hired for their job, from the steppes north of the Black Sea. These tribes figure in much of the history of both Greece and Persia. They served as allies or mercenaries with both sides in the Graeco-Persian wars. Racially they have been called the precursors of the Seljuk and Ottoman Turks, but the term Scyths seems to have been a blanket one. Some of them were the forerunners of the Huns, some of the Parthians and they seem to have been closely related to the tribes of the Iranian plateau.

They were all horse archers, with rigid laws and customs, bloodthirsty by habit and upbringing. They buried their kings and nobles surrounded with horse and slave sacrifices, and from some of their tombs we have recovered fantastically ornate combination bow-cases and quivers. They were primarily a nation of bronze users, due to the scarcity of iron in their home territory. They used bronze arrowheads exclusively and often armored their horses with light bronze plates. Herodotus relates that a king of the Scyths wished to know the number of his subjects. Under penalty of death he ordered each of his men to deposit one arrowhead at a designated point. When the tally was through, Ariantas, the king, ordered that the heap be converted into a huge cauldron, as a memorial to the might of the Scyths. Herodotus further records that the cauldron, with walls eighteen inches thick, held 5,400 gallons.

To seal a pact the horsemen cut their veins and mixed the blood with wine. Then each participant stuck an arrow into the mixture, and it was drunk by all. Several of the tribes practiced scalping, and it is not impossible to suppose that this custom was common all over Inner Asia. Another Scythian habit was to remove the skin from the right forearm and hand of a fallen enemy. The resulting hide was stretched over the victor's quiver as a decoration.

Of their methods of hunting, Herodotus mentions one, used by a specific tribe called Iyrkae: ". . . these also live by the chase in such a manner as I will show. The hunter climbs a tree, and there sits ambushed; for the trees grow thick all over the land; and each man has his horse at hand, trained to crouch upon its belly for lowliness' sake, and his dog; and when he marks the quarry from the tree, he shoots with the bow and mounts his horse and pursues after it, and the dog follows closely after."

Like so many of the Central Asiatic tribes, the Scyths used felt tents carried along on carts. Of one tribe, the Massagetae, Herodotus comments: "There when a man wants a woman, he takes his quiver and hangs it on her wagon and has intercourse with her freely."

While the Spartans were drilling and the rest of Greece was building and sculpturing and arguing, things were, as usual, moving in Asia. The steppes were spewing out tribes again. In the highlands of Iran another race had appeared, coming down from what we now surmise to have been the great steppes north and west of the Caspian. They called themselves many names—Medes, Persians, Aryans, Hyrcanians, Parthians, Drangians, Pactyans, Bactrians, Margians, Sogdians, Chorasmians and Sagartians. They were all cousins, and one branch of the family, which had been traveling with them, turned off to go down into India, along the Indus River valley, to form the Aryan invaders of the subcontinent.

North of them roamed other kindred tribes, the Scyths, or Sacae.

It is recorded, with tongue in cheek, that archery once settled the boundaries of Persian territory. After a small war between the semipastoral Persians and the still horse-borne Sacae a peace treaty guaranteed all the land northeast of Mt. Demavend to the Persians. This land was to extend as far as an arrow, shot from the mountain, would carry. At midnight a hero of the Persian fighters, Arish, climbed the mountain. He reached the top just before dawn and waited there for the first light. When it came he braced his bow and chose his best flight arrow. Then with a prayer to Ahura-Mazda he shot to the left of the rising sun. For hours the arrow flew until finally, at noon, it came to rest on the banks of the Oxus River, six hundred miles away. It is further recorded that the Sacae kept the treaty and the land was part of the territory of the Persians.

All these tribes lived a simple life, under a simple three-class society—warriors, free men and slaves. A fourth class were priests, who preached and practiced a simple religion, well suited to the pastoral life. The whole economy of the tribes centered around the great horse herds. Into the high plateau of Iran the tribes drifted, settling down where there was sufficient pasturage and displacing or absorbing the original inhabitants. Closest to the kingdoms of Assyria and Babylonia were the Medes, whose individual tribes inter-mittently came under the sovereignty of the Euphratean rulers.

With the passage of time, the Medes grew strong, united the tribes and set up their own small kingdom, acting as a thorn in the side of Assyria. Finally Cyaxares of Media combined forces with Nabopolassar of Babylon and the two monarchs destroyed Nineveh and the rest of the Assyrian Empire. They divided the territory amicably and each ruled his section, while Cyaxares extended his rule so as to make the Persians his vassals. Cyaxares kept Sacae bowmen in his court to act as archery instructors for both his own sons and those of the Median nobility.

This was roughly the situation when a petty king of Susiana, or Elam, decided to make a play for empire. Cyrus or Kurush, the Persian, went into open revolt against the son of Cyaxares, Astyages, and in the course of three years of war reduced the Median Empire and captured Astyages. Under the leadership of Cyrus, all the Persian tribes were welded into a nation and became the foremost world power of their day. In effect Cyrus established the first great empire. Although we count many previous rules as empires, Cyrus was the first to meld and blend his various subjects into a homogeneous whole. His military genius was supplemented with administrative ability so that he allowed his people a measure of self-government and treated them so wisely that they looked to the throne for protection, even though the incumbent might not be of their nationality or religious persuasion.

It is recorded that the Persians trained their sons from the fifth to the twenty-fifth years in three things only—riding, archery and truthtelling. Thus the strength of the Persian kings lay in their archer infantry. While the people continued to be great horse raisers, there was a natural tendency for the old "freemen" class to become agriculturalists, leaving the aristocracy to hold the great herds. However, despite the change from pastoralism, the common man retained his skill as an archer, using the same short, recurved bow that his sires had brought with them from the steppe country.

In actual battle formation, the mass of Persian archers went to the attack lightly armed. Only a hide-covered shield served as protection; for the rest they depended on the accuracy and volume of arrow flight to prevent the enemy from reaching their ranks. In fixed formation the shields were stuck in the ground in front of the ranks to serve as a partial wall, while the first row of archers knelt behind them. The second row was standing, and behind them, the back ranks contented themselves with firing in a high arc, so that their shafts passed over the heads of their comrades, falling among the attacking enemy. If that enemy had been able to reach the ranks of the archers, it would have created havoc—this happened in later battles—but unless they did, they were helpless facing the long-range fire of the Persians.

This dependence on the bow served the Persians well. In the course of their early empire they met and overcame the Medes, who fought in a similar fashion. The Median victory then was accomplished by means of bow over bow. What the actual deciding factor in this conquest was, history does not tell us, although it was probably discipline. But in the instance of the Lydian campaigns, where the Persians were again successful, it was a victory of the bow over mounted lancers. It must not be forgotten that the Persians themselves made extensive use of cavalry. In battle the cavalry would charge an enemy position to throw the lines into confusion and immediately retreat, leaving the disorganized foe prey to the arrows of the bowmen. This was particularly true with the Lydians, who might otherwise have ridden down the light archers. However, deflected by the attack of the Persian cavalry, Lydian men and horses fell to Persian arrows.

In conflict with Babylonians, Egyptians and Greeks, Persia proved the superiority of the bow over heavily armed, slow-moving infantry. Here again, only the rate of fire power by the archers saved them from annihilation. Had the bodies of hoplites and their opposite numbers in the other armies been able to get at the Persians, it would have spelled disaster. Aeschylus, in analyzing the Graeco-Persian Wars, viewed the entire series as a contest between bow and spear, leaving us with the conclusion that in the long run the spear is the superior weapon. While he is correct in his view that it was a "spear versus bow" contest, it is incorrect to assume that the spear is thereby proved the better weapon. Two great battles were the really decisive turning points in this series of wars. One, at Salamis, was a Greek naval victory and had a much greater effect on the morale of the Persian attack than did the land battle of Marathon. And it must be stressed that at Salamis, bows in the hands of Greek archers, aboard ship, were one of the deciding factors. Hoplites were ship-borne as well, but their effective range was limited to actual contact between ships. Until that actually took place, javelin men and archers were the only active forces. There was no such thing as naval tactics at Salamis. The conflict was hand to hand, with grappling and boarding being the prime objectives of the fleet commanders on both sides. While arrow fire could not stop the motion of a ship, it could and did sweep the decks clean of possible attackers or defenders.

Before we discuss the battle of Marathon in detail, it would be helpful to review some of the events which led up to it and the Graeco-Persian Wars generally. Cyrus, having overcome the Medes, spent most of the rest of his reign consolidating his holdings, or expanding to the east, without attempting European conquest. His successor, Cambyses, added Egypt to the Persian Empire, and in this connection there is one interesting archery tale.

Cambyses, from Egypt, sent ambassadors, who also served as spies, to the court of the King of Ethiopia. The king learned of their intentions and at their first official audience, presented them with a huge bow and bade them return to Cambyses with this message: "The King of the Ethiopians counsels the King of the Persians, when the Persians can draw a bow of this greatness as easily as I do, then to try with overwhelming odds to attack the long-lived Ethiopians; but until then, thank the gods who put it not in the minds of the Ethiopians to win more territory than they have." Obediently the ambassadors returned to Egypt with the bow and the message. And among all the Persians, no man could pull the bow, except Smerdis, the king's brother. He was able by struggling hard to pull it about three inches, but even that made Cambyses so angry he sent his brother home to Persia in a state of exile.

During his residence in Egypt, Cambyses displayed tendencies toward madness and during an argument with an adviser, gave ample proof of the fact. To the courtier Prexaspes, Cambyses said: "Yonder stands your son on the porch. Now if I shoot and pierce his heart, that will prove the Persians to be wrong. If I miss, then say that they are right and I out of my senses." Then the king strung his bow and let fly, hitting the boy. "He ordered servants to cut open the body and examine the wound; and the arrow being found in the heart, Cambyses laughed in great glee."

Smerdis briefly succeeded Cambyses, but the Persian emperor who undertook the first real assault of Greece was Darius. The political scene in Greece was so full of arguments between the various city-states that at one time or another almost all of them had begged the Persian ruler to intervene in their disputes. When Darius, at one point, asked who the Athenians were, he was told that they had been assisting Greek cities in Asia Minor in revolt against the throne. Then Darius called for his bow and, placing an arrow on the string, let it fly into the air, saying as the arrow left the string: "Grant me, Zeus, to revenge myself on the Athenians." This was the ruler who led his forces across the Hellespont to seek his vengeance and lashed the waves for delaying the crossing.

Perhaps no more varied an army has ever set forth in the history of the world. While many of the components came of their own will, other contingents moved only under the lash. Herodotus gives us an accounting of the army at the crossing. Without too many boring details and concerning ourselves only with the archers in the army, here is a partial listing: ". . . the Persians bore wicker shields for bucklers, their quivers hanging at their backs and their arms being a short spear, a bow of uncommon size and arrows of reed . . . The Medes as the Persians . . . (So too all the tribes of the

Iranian Plateau) . . . Bactrians armed with bows of cane
after the custom of their country . . . Sacae . . . they bore
the bow of their country . . . Indians . . . wore cotton
dresses and carried bows of cane and arrows also of cane
with iron at the point . . . Aryans . . . carrying Median
bows . . . Caspians . . . carried the cane bow of their country and the scimitar . . . Sarangians . . . they bore Median
bows and lances . . . Arabians . . . carried at their right
side longbows, which when unstrung bent backwards . . .
Ethiopians . . . had longbows made of the stem of the palm
leaf, not less than six feet in length. On these they laid short
arrows made of reed, and armed at the tip, not with iron,
but with a piece of stone, sharpened at the point, of the kind
used in engraving seals . . . Milyans . . . some of their
number carried Lycian bows. . . ." The Lycians are noted
in the enumeration of the naval forces, to the effect that
"they furnished fifty ships. Their crews wore greaves and
breastplates, while for arms they had bows of cornel wood
and reed arrows without feathers. . . ." A further note adds
that the Lycians were from Crete. We gather that, in most
cases, the cavalry was armed like the infantry listed above,
adding that the Arabians rode camels, giving us a glimpse
of camel-borne archers.

This polyglot, multicolored army marched down on
Greece. In certain states they were welcomed; in others they
simply overwhelmed any opposition they met. Only at the
Pass of Thermopylae did they encounter real defiance. The
story of the Spartan defense of the Pass is too well known
for retelling, but there is a grim joke about archery which
is supposed to have occurred on the last day of the gallant
fight. Somewhat unwillingly supporting the Spartans were
a small group of Trachinians, residents of the area. One of
them, looking at the Persian host that confronted them,
remarked: "Such is the number of the barbarians that when
they shoot forth their arrows, the sun will be darkened by
their multitude." The reply came from one of the hard-

bitten Spartans, Diences. "Our Trachinian friend brings us, then, excellent tidings. If the Medes darken the sun, we shall at least have our fight in the shade." This was Spartan courage in the face of impossible odds.

In the battle of Marathon the decisive factor was again not necessarily the superiority of the spear over the bow. It lay rather in a tactical shift, something which was brand-new in the military picture. Had the battle followed the prevailing pattern, history might have changed in a totally different way.

The background of Marathon was complicated in the extreme. Politics in Athens itself were so devious and the balance of power between parties so narrow, that a good part of the city was prepared to aid the Persians against their fellow citizens. The Persians landed along the Plain of Marathon, some twenty-odd miles northeast of Athens. A council of war in the city, held by the Polemarch Callimachus and ten generals, resulted in the dispatch of ten thousand Athenian hoplites through the mountain passes to meet the enemy on the plain. Messengers were sent to Sparta asking for help, and somewhere along the way the Athenians were joined by another one thousand men from the city of Plataea. When the combined Greek forces reached the mountains immediately above the plains, they moved down into a valley called the Funnel and waited. They were in a good spot since the land road to Athens passed through the Funnel. Having made camp, they set up picket lines and the war of nerves started. In effect both forces had their backs to a wall—the Greeks with mountains behind them and the Persians backing onto the sea.

The opposing forces waited. The Persians expected to hear that their political allies within the city were ready to move and the Athenians were waiting for Spartan reinforcements. Facing the eleven thousand Greeks were approximately double that number of Persians and while the Greeks were not cowards, such a preponderance of odds made them cautious. Finally the Persians broke the impasse. Their commander decided to put his troops back aboard ship and sail around to Athens, hoping to reach the city before the phalanx could make the march back through the mountains. Then, too, he expected that his allies within the city would be prepared to aid him on their own home ground. It was a calculated risk, since the Persians would of necessity have to defend themselves during the time it took to embark. But Persian troops had always been successful previously and the move began.

High in the mountain valley the Greeks saw the movement and correctly interpreted its meaning. Hoplites raced about donning their heavy armor and the body servants checked the stones for their slings. Down from the mountains they came, hurrying as fast as their armor would permit, with the long row of spears sticking out in front. When they came to the foot of the valley, they formed into the traditional phalanx form, with the men from Plataea on the left of the line. But this time there was one distinct difference in the makeup of the troops. Hitherto, as we have pointed out, all battles involving the phalanx had been head-on collisions, with no thought of turning or flanking. But this time, acting under Callimachus, the center was weak, with the men pulled out to strengthen the wings.

At a distance of about three quarters of a mile the two forces were in complete battle formation and advancing against each other. To the right of the Greeks was a small swamp and on their left, manned by the Plataeans, were hills coming closer to the sea. The Persian camp, with all its panoply, lay between these hills and the sea, while behind it, farther up the shore, was a big marsh. The fleet lay offshore from the Persian camp and as the troops moved closer, they tacked and hauled inshore to permit fast and easy boarding.

Closer and closer the enemies moved. A hail of arrows rose from the seaward side, dropping into the hedgehog of spears. Greek slingers cast their deadly missiles among the armorless Persians, and the air was full of battle. As the forces closed, the weakened center of the phalanx gave way while the Persians, from their straight iron front pushed into an arrowhead to take advantage of the Greek weakness. Then the flanks turned in on the advancing Persians and crushed them by sheer weight of numbers and armor. Callimachus, or more probably his chief military adviser, Militiades, had foreseen just such a move, and the wings were prepared. Battle had ceased to be simply a matter of brute force and tactics had been born. Over six thousand Persians perished on the Plain of Marathon and officers did well to rally the rest of the troops and get them aboard ship during the fierce fight. For none of the Persians and their allies wanted to stay and meet the iron-clad, victorious Greeks.

Turning, then, the Athenians and their allies marched, on the double, back to the city. But the Persians had had enough—the fleet cruised back and forth outside the harbor and the Athenians shouted challenges across the water. And they mocked the Spartans—for when they reached the city they found two thousand men from Sparta willing to help them. Athens rose in the estimation of the world, and the bow suffered a setback.

Throughout the course of the first Persian Empire, border wars against the Sacae or Scythians served to keep the army busy when not engaged in other wars. Cyrus, who had overthrown the Median yoke and established the empire, met his death while engaged in a punitive expedition against the Dahae and Massagetae in 529 B.C. The horse archers were under the leadership of a queen, Tomyris.

In a feinted withdrawal, which involved leaving a large quantity of wine in the deserted camp, Cyrus captured the son of the warrior queen, and when the youth's hands were freed he committed suicide. Then the rest of the Massagetae and Dahae set upon the Persians. Both sides fought with the

bow until the arrows were exhausted and it was too dangerous to pick up spent shafts. Hand-to-hand combat followed
in which the nomads finally prevailed, and Cyrus was among
the Persians slain. In vengeance for the trickery used to
capture her son, Tomyris had the body of Cyrus beheaded.
Then she caused another corpse to be skinned and the pelt
filled with blood. Into this gory tank she flung the head of
the dead emperor, crying to him to drink his fill of blood.

Darius, prior to his invasions of Greece, sent an expedi-
tionary force into the steppes, going through Thrace, to
teach the Sacae respect for the empire. Unfortunately, due
to a lack of geographical knowledge, the Persian forces overextended themselves and encountered great difficulty. The
army marched out into a veritable sea of grass and nearly got
lost. The farther from the base of supply they went, the more
devastating were the blows dealt by the Scythians. On the
horizon a group of riders would suddenly appear, racing
down on the supply trains. The riders, lying flat along their
saddles and drawing extremely short composite bows, shot
flight after flight of heavy arrows into the transport animals.
When the unit was stopped, the riders came in even closer
and fired the transport wagons, then turned and raced
away across the plains.

When the troops encountered bodies of horsemen, they
found that their own tactics didn't work, the riders didn't
want to close, but simply ranged around the army, outranging them with their bows and then disappearing. To add to
the Persian discomfiture, the Sacae burned the few crops
in the area of advance and added a final touch by polluting
the water supply. It was a deliberate scorched-earth policy.

According to Herodotus, Darius allowed himself to be
led farther and farther afield until finally one morning the
Persian camp awoke confronted by a horde of riders about a
mile off. Ever hopeful, Darius sent riders forward bearing
soil and water. In Persian terms, had the Sacae accepted, it

would have meant that they acknowledged the sovereignty of the Persians and at that late point Darius would probably have been satisfied.

The riders returned, without their earth and water, but carrying instead a present for Darius—a bird, a mouse, a frog and five arrows. Herodotus gives no reference to a written or oral message sent with this somewhat puzzling collection of objects. At length, one of the Persians, named Gobyrus (who seems to have been one of Darius' top commanders and may himself have been part Sacae) interpreted the riddle. In effect the Sacae leader said: "Unless you and your troops can turn into birds and fly from here, or if you can change into mice and burrow under the ground, or if you can become frogs and hide in the marshes, you will never escape from our lands but will die beneath our arrows."

Darius escaped, with some of his troops, but the way back through the burned and barren land was harder than the trip out. The Persians were too far from the base of supply, too overextended and confronted by horse archers possessing superior mobility and superior fire power.

The later Achaemenid emperors gradually softened. Like the small cities which sprang up and then fell to the outwall people, so empires are sapped of vitality and initiative by the very power and wealth which they gain at the onset. More and more the Persians came to depend on mercenaries, in many cases Greeks who sought a living away from the over-crowded peninsula and the islands.

One group of these Greek mercenaries stands out in history. Called the Ten Thousand Immortals, they enlisted under Cyrus the Younger in a short-lived revolt against his brother, Artaxerxes. When Cyrus was killed in battle and the Greek leaders slaughtered treacherously, the mercenaries fought their way through and across the largest part of the Persian Empire, to win their way to the sea and home. The Athenian, Xenophon, who started with the expedition in an unofficial capacity and later assumed command, has left us a simple and thrilling account of the entire trip. His work, the Anabasis, is still regarded as a classic text in warfare of this type and scattered throughout there are constant references to archery.

Speaking of the time immediately after the death of Cyrus, he says: "As for fuel they went forward a short distance from their line to the place where the battle was fought and used for that purpose not only arrows, many in number which the Greeks had compelled all who had deserted from the King to throw away, but also the wicker shields and the wooden Egyptian shields." The Persians had broken before a double-time charge of the phalanx, proving that in certain instances the lightly armed archer is certainly no match for heavy armored infantry.

Later during their retreat while constantly harassed by Persian forces, he mentions the plight of the two hundred Cretan bowmen who had accompanied Cyrus. "Mithridates appeared again, accompanied by about two hundred horsemen and by bowmen and slingers, exceedingly active and nimble troops . . . And the Greek rearguard while suffering severely, could not retaliate at all; for the Cretan bowmen not only had a shorter range than the Persians, but besides, since they had no armor, they were shut within the lines of the hoplites . . . Again the Persian horsemen, even while they were in flight, would inflict wounds by shooting behind them from their horses." It is interesting to note that the cast of the Persian bows must have been considerably greater than that of the famed Cretans.

Xenophon inquires and finds that in his command there are a certain number of Rhodian slingers. These men were as famed in the classic world for their skill with the sling as were the Cretans for their bowmanship. Xenophon orders the Rhodians to be armed with their traditional weapon and adds another valuable striking force to his small body of archers. Later when the Ten Thousand have stood off many attacks, they are marching in a hollow square while the Persians surround the flanks and the rear. Tissaphernes, the Persian commander, orders his slingers and archers to fire on the Greeks at will, hoping to break their lines. "But when the Rhodian slingers and the Cretan bowmen, posted at intervals here and there, sent back an answering volley, and not a man among them missed his mark, then Tissaphernes withdrew out of range with all speed . . . And the barbarians were no longer able to do any harm by their skirmishing at long range; for the Rhodian slingers carried farther than the Persians, farther even than the Persian bowmen. The Persian bows were also large and consequently the Cretans could make good use of all the arrows which fell into their hands; in fact they were continually using the enemy's arrows, and practiced themselves in long-range work by shooting them into the air." What the effective range of the Rhodian sling was, we cannot judge, but from Xenophon's description it would seem to have been a formidable weapon. From his observations about the arrows we can assume both sides were using similar bows, with the Persian weapons being either of heavier draw or of flatter trajectory. Both were recurved and composite—since this form of the bow was common throughout Grecian territory as well as Persia.

Farther on in their march, the Ten Thousand enter the country of the Carduchi, modern Kurdistan. The travel becomes difficult and treacherous because of steep mountain trails and they encounter the bowmen of that region. "Their only arms were bows and slings, and as bowmen they were very good. The bows they had were between four and five feet long and their arrows were of more than three feet. When they shot they put out the left foot and rested the bottom of the bow against it as they drew back the string. Their arrows went through shields and breastplates. When the Greeks got hold of any, they fitted them with straps and used them as javelins. In this type of country the Cretans were extremely useful. Stratocles, himself a Cretan, was their commander." Farther on into the lands of the Carduchi, Xenophon comments again on the penetrating power of the native arrows: "Here a gallant Spartan soldier, called Leonymus, was killed by an arrow which went into the side of his body through the shield and the jerkin, and Basias, the Arcadian, was also killed, shot clean through the head." The Carduchian bows seem as strong as any we find mentioned in antiquity, except for those of legendary kings and princes. And if the arrows were, in fact, later used as javelins, we can only suppose that they would be of an almost improbable diameter, suited perhaps to the draw of a two-hundred-pound bow. The disproportion between bow length and shaft length would indicate that the hill tribes had been influenced in their design by the Babylonians and Hittites.

Xenophon and his men finally returned to Greece, via the Dardanelles, drawing to a close the most colorful account of mercenary warfare in the history of the ancient world.

At home the city-states continued, with first one league and then another occupying the leading position. The culmination of the arguments came in the Peloponnesian War, 431-404 B.C. The principal protagonists were Athens and Sparta, with their allies. In the great chronicle of that war, written by Thucydides, we find that archery was part and parcel of warfare in Greece at the time, with the archer still a potent force in naval victories, for he cites not only their use aboard ship, but also notes one occasion when sixty hoplites and a handful of archers successfully repelled a landing attempt by forty-three ships. References to the bow and its effectiveness occur throughout the books, with both sides insuring an ample supply of bowmen. Two events of special interest are mentioned. One is the attack on the city of Plataea, where Thucydides records the use of fire arrows by the attackers and the defenders countering with wet hides slung along the woodwork. The second is perhaps the only instance on record where the arrow was used as an instrument of suicide. A group of Athenians are besieged within a strong building by a force of Corcyraeans. Unable to gain access to the building itself, the attackers get onto the roof and tear open holes, through which they shoot at the Athenians below. The imprisoned Athenians, seeing no hope for escape, begin to commit suicide, many of them thrusting into their own throats arrows which have been shot at them.

The outcome of the Peloponnesian Wars was the loss of leadership by both Sparta and Athens. Then a new power came into Greece from the north.

There in the highlands lived a tribe called the Macedonians. They were mountaineers and herdsmen, tough, self-sufficient and crude, by Hellenic standards. Because of this very crudeness they often trod on the toes of their more effete neighbors and in consequence one of their kings spent much of his youth as a hostage in the city of Thebes, which at the time was the strongest and richest of the city-states. With a keen eye, the young prisoner watched the drills and maneuvers of his Theban hosts and when he finally returned to his beloved homeland he set about building a new army, based on his observations but with his own additions.

Because of the size of the Macedonian plains, the nation had already developed the finest cavalry in Greece. Now, Philip, the king, was determined to combine the cavalry with the traditional Doric phalanx. He had noted in Thebes the perfection of the mercenaries, at the same time realizing that their motivations were based on monetary considerations. If he could establish a body of hoplites who had the same technical perfection, but who were moved by loyalty, he would have the perfect arm to combine with his horsemen. So the Macedonian army was forged, not only in theory, but in battle practice. Philip fought up and down, back and forth, now with allies, now alone. He married a woman reputed to be a witch, who gave him a son. He lost an eye, he limped and one arm was useless, but he left his son an army which conquered the world.

In essence, the Macedonian army, under both Philip and

his son Alexander, was made up of many units. The phalanx was still the center, with the spear now reaching a length of twenty feet. Unwieldy though these spears were, they lengthened the security of the mass, much as a rifle with a longer range covers its user more effectively. Equipped with these superspears the phalanx, composed of six sections of five thousand men each, formed a base about which the cavalry could work. Philip never intended the phalanx to be a highly mobile unit.

On either of its flanks were the heavy cavalry units—on the left the Thessalians and on the right the Companions—who were drawn from the aristocracy of Macedonia and who were, by right and tradition, the actual companions of the king. To protect the phalanx even further, Philip put wedges in between the main body and the heavy cavalry. Again: on the left, Thracian javelin men and on the right the hypaspists or shield-bearers. These were heavy infantry but used for fast attack, unlike the slow-moving hoplites. If a cavalry attack by the Companions was successful, they served as a striking force to damage the enemy's front ranks and in normal fighting they guarded both the right flank of the phalanx and the left flank of the Companions. Farther out on the left, past the Thessalians, was another body of horsemen, lightly armored and used for swift diverting attacks. On the far side of the Companions was a similar group of light cavalry and beyond them, at the extreme right of the Macedonian line, were the archers, usually Cretans, who were Alexander's favorites. With this essential grouping of troops and using a number of attack plans, Philip won his wars and Alexander won his world.

Alexander was not content in Greece, Macedonia and Thrace, but crossed over into Asia and made his way as far as India. In the course of his travels he changed his battle order on many occasions, adapting to the needs or the instant, but the hard core of his army always was made up of the phalanx and the Companions. In time, due to a lack of Macedonians and their allies, he was forced to substitute from among his new subjects insofar as light cavalry, infantry and archers were concerned; but his army was distinctive at all times—it never lost a battle.

Twice this golden-haired warrior came near defeat and both times archery was a large factor in the battle. An account of Alexander's conquests is a book in itself, in fact it has served as the basis for many, but our interest lies principally in these two. One occurred in Central Asia, north of the Himalayas, where the young god-king (his new subjects and even his own men were convinced that he was of divine birth) was attempting to establish a permanent empire, with cities he hoped to colonize with Greeks. But before such work could be successfully undertaken it was necessary to subdue all the possible rebellious tribes. Pursuing this course of armed pacification and colonization, Alexander and the army arrived on the banks of the Syr Darya, called the River of Sands. Here he halted and began the construction of what was to be the northernmost of the cities.

Across the river the Scythians or Sacae began to gather. They watched in open wonder as the trained engineers of Alexander's army supervised the rapid construction of stone walls for the town. Their wonder changed to mocking and they spent long hours grazing their horses and shooting arrows across the water to annoy the Greeks. At that range, fortunately for the builders, most of the shafts fell short. In the meantime Alexander received word that the city of Samarkand was under siege by the chief rebel of the area, an ex-army officer of the now defunct Persian Empire. Alexander immediately dispatched a relief force consisting of 2,400 men, including a squadron of the Companions to raise the siege.

The Greeks had ample time to observe the enemy across the water. Hairy, bearded men they were, with long blond mustaches and fur garments which protected them against the bitter steppe winds. They carried deeply recurved bows and long straight swords and their mocking cries carried across the river. Finally the city was finished and Alexander prepared for the attack.

He chose this time for a series of games and contests among his men, which served three purposes. The first was to raise the flagging spirits of the Macedonians, while the second and third were just as practical. By so doing, he confused the Sacae, who had had no previous contact with an enemy acting in this fashion, and his seemingly absurd commands gave his men a partial screen for their preparations.

Along the banks of the river the engineers set up a row of heavy ballistae, designed to fire light javelins. There is some argument as to whether these were the precursors of the modern crossbows, but whatever their name, they could and did lay down an accurate and heavy fire of javelins. Meanwhile rafts had been built and on the assault wave Alexander placed a mixed force of slingers, archers and light infantry. The men launched the rafts out into the muddy, swirling waters and the Scythians on the far bank loosened their quivers. To them this was going to be good sport, the Scythian equivalent of shooting sitting birds. At this exact moment the ballistae took over and the heavy spears began to land among the massed horsemen. Men and horses dropped in confusion as the spears went through light armor and heavy leather clothing. Prudently the Scythians withdrew out of range, allowing the first wave to land, comparatively unmolested. Dragging themselves ashore, they spread out in a screen formation covering the landing of the cavalry and the phalanx on the next wave of rafts.

When the heavier troops were ashore, Alexander ordered a mixed formation forward, in all probability the men who had formed the assault wave. They went up cautiously, shooting as they moved, but unfortunately, shooting at a target which wasn't there. Then the Scyths returned and cut the forward screen to ribbons, then wheeled and went off again.

Slowly, ponderously the phalanx went forward, to the

brazen accompaniment of the war trumpets, which had been sounding since before the first rafts hit the water. The Sacae rode round and round in clockwise fashion, cutting swathes in the Macedonians and fleeing before the heavy Companions or the Thessalians could move. Alexander had for once brought himself and his men into a situation with which they couldn't, for the moment, cope. Slowly the phalanx halted and the trumpets ceased blaring. Up and down the line the voices of the noncoms broke the silence, shouting commands as the Sacae came in again, shrilling war cries. Never before had the phalanx met such a foe—against all rules of warfare they refused to hold still, refused to serve as a target. Only the steadfast discipline of the veterans kept the entire Graeco-Persian force from complete rout.

Alexander had been in the first wave and he was now in the lead of the field. Hastily he rallied a group of mixed cavalry and sent them out on one flank of the immobilized phalanx. After them he sent the hypaspists as a rear guard. On Bucephalus, his famous stallion, Alexander raced across the front of the phalanx and assumed command of the Companions. The mixed cavalry had not actually contacted the Scyths, but their forward thrust had halted the wheeling of the enemy. Then at the head of the Companions, Alexander charged out from the opposite wing so that the two cavalry forces moved together, pinching the Sacae in the middle and trying to drive them in toward the phalanx. Sensing the trap, the horse archers turned away from the center of the battle, heading for the open plains, with both bodies of Macedonian horse in full pursuit. Alexander had won another battle and this time his tactics were completely devised on the spot, vindicating his veterans' faith in his supremacy as a tactician.

With the battle won, the Macedonians returned to the new city and almost immediately proceeded to the south toward Samarkand. Alexander, weakened by wounds and a recurrent fever, was carried in a litter after the pursuit of the Scythians, but when couriers told him that the relief of

Samarkand had failed, he rose from his bed and led the flying column which actually relieved the city. The 2,400 men he sent south had been trapped at a river crossing by Scythians and wiped out. The tactics of the horse archers were eminently suited to their land. Only the military genius of Alexander had saved the main force from annihilation on the banks of the Syr Darya.

As the army marched forward into Asia, the rank and file grew weary. They had been away from home for more than seven years. They idolized their leader, but they rebelled at some of the eastern customs which he had adopted, and they longed for the plains and mountains of home. Only the phalanx and the Companions were left of the original army and it was shot full of new levies who had marched out from Macedonia each spring. The others were dead, gone home or colonizing in the cities they'd left in their wake. New allies rode with them, Bactrian and Scythian horsemen—blood brothers to the enemy at the River of Sand. Even the Companions carried a high percentage of Persians in their muster list. And so grumbling, the phalanx went, still following the star of Alexander.

Among the native rulers who had received the Macedonians with open arms in India was the Rajah Omphi. He was treated as an equal by the emperor, and the men grumbled even more at losing the right to pillage his land. Still the army marched east. Even the Companions and the king's bodyguard complained that the rajah was more favored than they. When they came to the end of his lands they were faced by two obstacles—the river Jhelum in full flood and the army of the Paurava kings facing the river. Paurava was the tradition enemy of Omphi, and Alexander had pledged his army to break that enemy, once and for all.

The enemy army seemed easy to the battle-hardened troops, but its specialty and real danger were huge war elephants. The Macedonians were faced with trial by water and animals. Some authorities hold that Alexander should have waited for the flood-swollen river to subside—it would only have been a matter of a few days—but the king was tired. Tired, physically and mentally, for not only had he led his men in every engagement and every pursuit, he insisted more and more in making the command a one-man operation. He refused to delegate authority—every detail, no matter how petty, must come to his personal attention. The strain of the long campaigns was telling on the leader more than on the men. Exhausted, unreasonable, intent on the destiny he dreamed for himself, he determined to cross the river without delay.

Applying psychology, Alexander staged raids on enemy territory lying on the west bank of the river, brought in huge supplies of food and simulated attacks through the river. Then in the middle of the night, leaving a cover of men in camp, he took the main force eighteen miles to the north and crossed the river just at dawn. So far, the move had gone without a hitch but when they finally made the far bank they alerted Paurava sentries.

Plowing on through ground that was fetlock-deep in mud, the Macedonians moved south along the riverbank. Scouts brought word that the enemy was just ahead, and a detachment of light cavalry moved out for interception. Riders soon returned to report that the force had found only two thousand men, who had quickly been demolished. Then Alexander was faced with finding the main body of the enemy. Realizing that the progress of the foot soldiers would be slow because of the mud, he took the cavalry and again headed south. When he came on the enemy his tactical position was bad. On a section of high ground stood the war elephants, two hundred of them, stationed one hundred feet apart. In the intervals stood tall, brown-skinned archers and behind the archers were infantry and javelin men. The cavalry was at an impasse because of the horses' innate fear of elephants. All that Alexander could do was wait for the support of the phalanx before he attacked the Indian cavalry.

When the hoplites and hypaspists arrived, they instantly went into battle formation, facing the wall of elephants and archers. Arrian, the historian, says that the bows facing the phalanx that day, from between the elephants, were so strong that to be bent, one end had to rest on the ground. Their arrows flew with such force that they easily penetrated the body armor of the phalanxmen and the hypaspists.

Alexander left the infantry to their own devices. His cavalry had recently been augmented by contingents of horse archers from the steppe and he was eager to try them in battle, this time on his side. Drawing the Companions slowly from the front of the Indian cavalry, he feigned a retreat, at the same time sending the Scythians around in a wide sweep to take the foe in the rear. Jammed between the light, but hard-riding rear attack and the heavily armored Companions, the Indians gave ground slowly and then fought practically to the last man.

The phalanx and the hypaspists, left to themselves, began a slow march toward the wall of elephants, suffering heavy losses from the huge arrows which whished into their ranks. And as the wall of spears moved forward, the wall of flesh moved out to meet it. Even a twenty-foot spear is scant defense against an elephant, but somehow the Macedonians won the day. Our only explanation for this remarkable feat is that probably javelins thrown by the hypaspists accounted for the mahouts on the war elephants. Each time an elephant hit the phalanx the line would buckle. Even discipline can't cope with a squealing, charging bulk of that size moving at fast trot. The great feet came down on the Greeks, and their tusks, sheathed in metal, swung like bloody scythes through the ranks. Even with their riders gone, the beasts backed slowly from the battle, seeming to sense that their retreat spelled death.

Finally Alexander finished off the cavalry and returned to the phalanx, which he re-formed. At this point, the remainder of the Macedonians crossed the river and took up the pursuit of the Paurava army. It was Alexander's last battle—the Macedonians took several hill towns for him after that, but then they demanded to go home and Alexander yielded.

Back in the area of the Tigris and the Euphrates which he had chosen as his capital, the Emperor of the World released the Macedonian veterans and turned to the civil administration of his realm. Shortly afterward, while planning new conquests and explorations, the greatest man of his age died, the victim of malaria.

After his death the empire fell apart. The bodyguard generals split the parts and gnawed at the bones. Macedon lapsed into a pathetic apathy, living on the glory of Philip and his son. Seleucus founded the short-lived Seleucid Dynasty in Persia and only Ptolemy Lagus, in Egypt, fathered a long line of rulers. Shortly after, another race of archer horsemen overran Iran and the rest of Alexander's empire to form their own, the Parthian.

5

Archery in the Roman Era

UNQUESTIONABLY ROME WAS THE GREATEST MILITARY POWER
of her era. Her conquests stretched from Spain to Persia and
from England to Egypt. Her senators, her generals and her
emperors are more familiar to us than her poets. Rome was
never a nation of archers, in the sense that the bow was used
by young and old, or that it was common to all classes. In
fact, in the history of the fabled legions, the bow seems only
to have played a decisive part when the legions themselves
suffered sorely. There are few references to Roman archers in
the annals of the state, and where we do find any mention of
the bow, it is most often in connection with auxiliaries and
mercenaries serving with or under the Roman eagles.

It is not the purpose of this book to go into the roots of
Rome—as a struggling young state, a militant republic or a
glorious, though decadent, empire. This is a history of the
bow, not of nations, and because Rome was so largely independent of the bow, our consideration of her will be,
perforce, a cursory one.

The most common conception of Roman history is that of
a nation of sturdy farmer-soldiers, under the leadership
of a senate, which in turn gave place to a vast military empire, administered by a series of emperors more famed for
their eccentricities than their abilities. As for what came before the Republic, most of us are content to believe the
Romulus-Remus legend without much question.

Rome was in fact an autocratic rule imposed on any number of small kingdoms, most of whose names are lost to all but the Latin scholar. Because of the peculiar nature of its growth, there was seldom a period when the Roman regime enjoyed great stability and as a result it depended for its very existence on armed might. With the subjugation of the various small states and constant border war, Rome became a nation of militaristic traders, carrying not only the eagles of the legions but a pattern of conquer-and-colonize to the ends of the then known world.

In the original Roman constitution there is a reference to archery. In ordering the defenses of the city—and here we must remember that this Rome was one small city, not a great republic—it is recorded that the "arquites" were to act as supports for the "quirites." The arquites, who later were known as "sagittarii," were those "who go with the bow," while the term quirites was a loftier designation—"the spear-armed warriors." The distinction against archers is one which remained throughout Roman history. Even the "equites" or "horse-mounted warriors," who were to become the elite of later Roman society, were not horse archers. And the supporting arquites soon faded from the Roman picture, for shortly after the original reference, a constitutional reform occurred under Servius Tullius, in which all mention of the arquites is omitted.

There was in Rome, at one point, a monument erected to honor one T. Flavius Expeditus, an archery instructor. The tribute called him "Doctorus Sagittarius" or arrow doctor and from this it seems safe to assume that archery may well have been popular as a sport for children and young men, but it was not a military weapon in Roman eyes. Not until the end of the Spanish wars did archery play any substantial role in Roman military history. Then, under Scipio Aemilianus, mercenary archers from Crete were a deciding factor in the defeat of the Numantines in Spain.

As Rome continued her policy of expansion, the value of

archery was certainly recognized by Roman generals. Ever astute to exploit the talents of their subjects and neighbors, the generals of the legions used bowmen among their auxiliaries wherever and whenever possible. In the *Commentaries on the Gallic War* of Julius Caesar, we find that wily campaigner using both Cretan and Numidian archers in his long fight against the Belgae. The continued use of Cretans at this comparatively late date is ample proof that the islanders were continuing to use the bow as ably as they had in the Classical period. The Numidians, who had first come into contact with the Romans during the Punic Wars, were excellent warriors in every sense and were specially skilled in handling long bows. Their reed arrows, often poison-tipped, were a constant source of terror to the Teutonic tribes.

The Numidians had earlier proved their worth at the battle of Zama, against the Carthaginians. The Carthaginians often used Numidians as mercenaries, or even slave troops, against the Romans, but at Zama the tribes were on the side of the men from the Tiber. Their flanking arrow attack against Hannibal broke the heart of the Punic resistance and resulted in the final defeat and destruction of Carthage. Little wonder, then, that Julius Caesar rated them among the most valuable of his auxiliaries.

Perhaps the greatest single defeat ever suffered by Roman forces came at the hands of archers. In the year 54 B.C., Marcus Licinius Crassus was one of the three men who ruled Rome as a member of the First Triumvirate. Crassus gained his position solely through judicious use of his wealth, and at no time had he ever made a name for himself as a soldier. Nevertheless, when it fell his lot to take over the administration of Rome's eastern provinces, he became inflamed by tales of conquest and determined to annex Parthia, which lay to the east of Roman Syria. The Parthians were Asiatics, closely akin to the Scythians and perhaps to the Medes and Persians, although there is some doubt as to whether or not they were Aryan. No matter what their bloodstream, they had succeeded to the rule of what had been the Seleucid Empire and represented the second greatest military power in the world.

Crassus was ill-advised to attempt the conquest of such a people, but he was firmly convinced of the invincibility of the legions. Tales of Parthian wealth inhibited any common sense he may have felt and blinded him to his own incapability as a military commander. To effect his conquest he took with him seven legions, four thousand cavalry and a mixed body of four thousand archers and slingers. He readily accepted guides from the local Bedouin tribes, who were actually in Parthian pay, and thereby exposed himself to attack in the worst possible manner.

The Parthians were nomadic in origin and like almost all of the nations and tribes which have risen in steppe regions, were first-rate horsemen and even better archers. Since Parthia had already established itself as an empire, the use of cavalry had evolved from the primitive, so that opposing the Romans were two distinct bodies of warriors. The first were the traditional horse archers, lightly clad, carrying a short, strong, deeply recurved bow, with a hit-and-run method of attack. The second body was composed of mailed horsemen. This second division also carried bows for long-range work, but their most effective method of fighting was close at hand, where their long lances enabled them to make short work of their opponents. We somehow imagine that fully armored horsemen, mounted on equally well-armored horses are indigenous to the Middle Ages, but many Asiatic tribes were adept at this form of warfare, and some even went so far as to engage in single combat centuries before the medieval tournaments. Such was the body of troops opposing Crassus.

The Roman banker, for such he had been, allowed the legions to be drawn into rapid pursuit of the Parthians, who were feigning retreat. Crassus' opposite number was Surenas, a young man who stood second to the Parthian emperor in command of the nation. Surenas at the time was still less than thirty years old, and although by repute he painted his face, there seems to be no doubt as to his masculinity, for he brought into battle with him a train of two hundred concubines.

Surenas seems to have been one of the first generals really to assess the value of archery in war. We have seen that the bow is a superb weapon, used judiciously. It could be adapted to both offensive and defensive purposes with equal facility and it was a weapon which recognized no economic or socio-economic levels. Where wood existed, bows could be made cheaply. Where no wood existed, the bowyer found acceptable substitutes. And neither bows nor arrows are dependent in any great part on metal production—thereby releasing their users from the necessity of holding or having access to metal. There was, and is, however, one great drawback to the use of archery as an offensive weapon, and that is the question of supply. Time and again in both ancient and modern chronicles we find bowmen forced to sally out onto the battlefield to recover spent shafts in order to sustain any rate of fire.

Surenas, recognizing this shortcoming of the bow, ordered up with his troops a body of over one thousand camels, which served as a munitions train. The camels were loaded with spare arrows so that the Parthian archers, being completely mobile in their attack, could resupply themselves with shafts even in the midst of battle. Nor did this "reloading" matter in the course of fighting, for their hit-and-run tactics did not demand that they occupy and hold any given spot. As one body ran short of arrows they simply retreated and drew more ammunition, while their places in the constantly shifting line of battle were taken by other horsemen.

Crassus met the Parthians near the river Belik and found that Surenas had taken advantage of the wooded slopes to improve his position. When the two bodies of men made contact, the legions immediately formed up into the traditional hollow square, with the slingers and archers enclosed and with the cavalry on the flanks of the square. Such a formation, even without the mounted wings, had been responsible for many Roman victories, based as it was on the principle of an immovable wall of heavily armed men. Against these living walls many tribes and nations had flung themselves, only to find that iron Roman discipline and iron Roman weapons were more than a match for disorganized courage and heroically inspired gallantry.

At first the Romans were hopeful that the Parthians would follow an accepted pattern and charge the square, but the riders stopped well out of range of the Roman javelins and began to fire volley after volley of arrows into the close-packed ranks. The archers and slingers enclosed in the square returned the fire, but being both outranged and outnumbered by the enemy, their effect was barely noticeable. From a strategic standpoint the Romans were poorly placed, since the superior Parthian cavalry commanded all communications. And tactically they were at an even greater disadvantage because their weapons were all of a close-order nature (even the *pila* or javelins were for extremely short-range work) and such weapons must eventually succumb to those wielded from a distance, unless the combat is at close quarters. The entire pattern of Roman warfare was based on the invulnerability of the concentrated position—ideal for the defense of towns or for campaigns where legion tactics were foreseeably advantageous. Alexander, confronted by a similar situation, had had the advantage of large bodies of mixed cavalry, of light armed mobile infantry and above all of supreme tactical ability. Crassus had none of these and his use of horse particularly shows hesitation and inadaptability. Had he used his cavalry as a cover for the archers and slingers, the legion might have been able to entrench itself, but standing on the riverine plains of Belik, the Roman forces were vulnerable in the extreme. Here danger increased as the ranks closed for the very reason that there was less room for Parthian arrows to miss. As one historian has said, "Imagination can hardly conceive a situation in which all the military advantages were more on the one side, and all the disadvantages more thoroughly on the other."

When the Parthians first began to deluge the square with arrows, the officers and men held fast, sure that the attack would dwindle for lack of arrow ammunition, but the munitions camels came into play and the arrow fire continued without ceasing. Even Crassus recognized the seriousness of the situation at this point and ordered skirmishers out, to augment the cavalry and to give further protection to the arrow-riddled legions. The Roman auxiliaries, archers and slingers both, came out from the square but were just as promptly driven back into its safety. Hopelessly outnumbered and totally outranged, their movement represented a tactical loss to the Romans. Had Crassus used them as skirmishers, immediately on establishing contact with the Parthians, it would have at least offered a delaying movement, but when they did come out into the open, they offered sure targets for the horse archers.

Then Crassus ordered charges by units out of the square walls. Centuries of men dashed out from the legion ranks, moving at a brisk trot, trying vainly to hold the enemy. Each time the archers raced away from the moving ranks, firing over their shoulders as they fled, and each time the legionaries retreated, unable to establish contact. The ranks of the centuries were thinned by arrows which drove with such force that they penetrated shields and breastplates, wreaking havoc with the shield wall. Crassus decided that attack in force was the only solution to the problem and ordered his own son, Publius, to take as many men as he needed and break through the Parthian concentration.

Publius had been trained in Gaul under Julius Caesar, and for the attack chose to take with him a body of one thousand Celtic horsemen, who had come with him from Gaul. In addition, the striking force consisted of five hundred archers and four thousand legionaries. The Celts drew off while the legions formed up in columns and the archers went wide on the flanks. Publius ordered the charge sounded and the troops moved forward, men and horses at a fast trot.

The Parthians fled before the Roman advance, and in the square, the rest of Crassus' men reformed their ranks and held their ground. Scattered groups of Parthians still ranged about the shield wall, but the main body had drawn off in Publius' van. But Surenas' retreat had been feigned and as soon as young Publius took the bait, the trap closed. Out of sight of the main body of Romans, Surenas brought his heavy cavalry into position, forming a wall against which the Celts threw themselves. Unable to break through the armored cavalry, the Gauls turned, only to face wave after wave of horse archers who rode past, riddling them with arrows. In the meantime, the legionaries retreated to a little hill and there made their last stand, behind their shield wall.

Of the six thousand men under Publius, five hundred were taken prisoner and the rest killed. The archers broke and fled, with the Parthians riding them down like so many rabbits. Publius himself was slain and his head thrown back into the hollow square, to tell the Romans of his fate. Then the main force of Parthians attacked, this time with the armored lancers in the fore. Surenas, having softened his melon by arrow fire, now sought to split it with the iron wedge of his shock troops.

The archers moved back from the front of battle, but still close enough so that their fire was effective. Arrows from their bows continued to pour down into the ranks of the legions even as the heavy cavalry moved in for the kill. The impetus of the riders was such that often one lance would impale two Romans.

Only nightfall saved the Romans from total destruction. According to their custom the Parthians drew off and made camp some distance away, allowing the battle-weary Romans time to slip away in the darkness. Behind him Crassus left four thousand wounded men, who were promptly massacred by the Parthians on the following morning.

Retreating, the Romans were constantly harassed, and Crassus fell on the parley ground near a spot called Sinnaca. Of his officers, only the quaestor Longinus Cassius escaped with a body of five hundred horse. Ten thousand Romans were taken into the regions of Central Asia and there settled as serfs. Of the original forty thousand men who started with Crassus, on the march to Carrhae, only the serfs and Cassius' few lived to tell of the great defeat. Archery, as an arm with both extreme mobility and heavy, sustained fire power, had devastatingly demonstrated its superiority over the slow-moving, iron-clad, iron-disciplined legions.

Nevertheless we must not overestimate the bow as a military weapon, for it, like every other arm, has its limitations. Circumstances must be such as to give the bow a tactical advantage before it develops its fullest potential in war. Without the necessary advantage, the bow, like any other weapon, loses its value and does not achieve full scope. To illustrate the point, let us look ahead to the period in Roman history which followed the breakup of the First Triumvirate, when Julius Caesar and Gnaius Pompeius brought their civil war to a head at Dyrrhachium in Greece.

In this instance both sides were well equipped, both with legionaries and with auxiliaries of every sort. Both armies were well used to the Roman type of warfare, both offensive and defensive. Records show that Pompey, as he is more commonly known, numbered three thousand archers in the forces under his command, and it is safe to assume that Caesar had a comparable force.

In the constant shuffling for position which occurred during this campaign one incident proves the uselessness of bows and arrows under certain circumstances. Caesar ordered a single cohort of men to hold a redoubt situated on a small hill. At that juncture the redoubt was valuable to both sides,

and Pompey launched a full-scale attack to gain its possession. At dawn four full legions came into action, throwing
waves of men up against the strong point. Thrown back, they
stood off while Pompey ordered his archers to reduce the hill
to submission. Shock and close-range missile fire in the form
of javelins having failed, Pompey apparently expected that
long-range missile fire, arrows, would succeed. Thirty thousand arrows were shot into the redoubt, without dislodging
the one hundred defenders. There is no more conclusive
evidence in military history of the inadequacy of the bow in
attacking a set of permanent fortifications when they are well
manned. Caesar relieved the cohort with two full legions
later in the day.

This primary drawback of archery as a weapon against
permanent installations is accompanied by one other. Light
armed archers were never a match for heavy armored infantry if the archers were forced to remain stationary, except
under certain specified conditions. If the archers had good
discipline and an unlimited amount of ammunition they
could repel infantry attack, could in other words prevent
shock tactics from taking effect. Once infantry, or cavalry,
had closed the gap between themselves and the archers, it
was the latter who suffered. If the archer had, as in the case of
the Parthians, the added factor of mobility, the slow-moving
infantryman with his hand-to-hand weapons was at the
mercy of the archer. But immobility or a lack of protection
placed the archer in a peculiarly weak position.

In the same campaign, in and around Dyrrhachium, Pompey and his aristocratic supporters were finally vanquished.
The tide of battle might have gone otherwise, had Pompey's
three thousand archers been mounted, disciplined or otherwise protected. As it was, in the deciding battle of the campaign, they and their slinger counterparts were lost through
the defeat of their protectors, the aristocratic cavalry.

Both Caesar and Pompey depended on a face-to-face fight

between the legions for the main battle, much as the Greek forces had met with their phalanxes. Pompey had hoped, however, to disorganize and demoralize Caesar's center by a heavy concentration of arrows and sling missiles. To gain this objective, Pompey threw out his archers on one wing, supposedly protected by cavalry and with a clear field of fire at the republican center.

Caesar, aware of Pompey's motive, brought his own cavalry from its place on his wings and threw them against the aristocrats, who crumpled after two short, vicious charges. With the cavalry screen gone, Caesar's horse then rode down the archers and slingers. With both the cavalry and the archer-artillery disposed of, Caesar was then free to flank Pompey with his horse and finally rout the aristocratic forces.

The very fact that archers in any Roman force were auxiliaries and not first-line troops, mitigated against them. If Roman command had placed more emphasis on the bow as a weapon and had drilled and disciplined their archers to a degree anything like that which obtained in the legion, the bow would have been infinitely more effective. Had Pompey's archers been adequately led and organized, they would have been able to repel the attack of Caesar's cavalry —if we grant that they had a sufficient number of arrows. But this failure to rely on archers was universal in the Rome of this period, and Dyrrhachium is not an isolated instance, but merely serves to typify the treatment of archers and their potential in the days of the Republic and the Early Empire. The bowmen were simply an unimportant segment of the *auxilia,* useful for skirmishing and harassing movements. There are no records which show battles lost or won by Roman archers, unless we attribute the defeat of Pompey to the loss of his bowmen. We get some idea of the number of archers used in Roman forces, on a proportionate basis, by examining the men involved in the battle of Philippi, which came after the assassination of Julius Caesar. Here there were twenty footmen and three horsemen for every archer. Obviously, infantry were the favored branch of the Roman military.

Mark Anthony, rankled by the loss of the eagles of Crassus at Carrhae, once attempted to conquer Parthia. Since he was a far abler soldier than Crassus, his preparations were better made and his motivations seem to have been from a patriotic standpoint. Yet in spite of his ability and his steps of precaution, Anthony nearly lost his life in the attempt.

He split his forces in two—the first, consisting largely of legionaries, moved with Anthony himself and settled down to the siege of Praaspa, capital of Media. The baggage train, siege engines and slow-moving troops came after, commanded by Oppius Statianus, one of Anthony's junior officers. Again, Parthian horse archers challenged Roman might, and this time the entire siege train was lost, along with ten thousand men, including the commander, Statianus. The tactics which had overwhelmed Crassus were equally effective against Statianus—first the withering, endless rain of armor-piercing arrows and then the attack by horsemen in full armor.

Anthony was unable to sack Praaspa without his siege equipment and his foraging parties were being cut to pieces by Parthians, so that food began to run short in the camp. Resigning himself to retreat, Anthony gradually made his way back into Roman territory. The only factor which saved the march from becoming a complete rout was the presence, in the Roman ranks, of a large body of Rhodian and Illyrian slingers. While the Roman auxiliary archers were outranged by the Parthian bowmen, the effective range of the slingers was such that they were able to stave off partially the Parthian attacks. During the march of 270 miles, Anthony lost over a third of his men to the horse archers and would have lost more had it not been for the slingers. Anthony is said to have recalled the retreat of the Ten Thousand under Xenophon through the same country centuries before, when they too were protected from mounted bowmen by the efforts of Rhodian slingers.

With the passage of time, changes were quite naturally effected in the composition of the Roman army. The backbone of the forces remained the legion, but more and more *auxilia* poured into the ranks, and we find Augustus, the first emperor, officially defining their position. His law states that all men of the actual legion were to be Roman citizens, while the *auxilia* remained apart. Since Roman citizenship was highly prized, we can be sure that archers, since they were still *auxilia*, continued to be looked down on, from a military standpoint.

Yet archers were coming to form more and more of a part of the over-all military organization. Quintilius Varus, proconsul in Germany, was defeated near Ems, in an area of Germany called the Teutoburger Wald, largely because his archers were ineffective. Dio, in his *Roman History* says of the battle, "The wet and the woods stopped them from going forward and even from standing securely, and moreover deprived them of the use of their weapons. For they could not handle their *bows,* or their javelins with any success, nor for that matter, their shields, which were thoroughly soaked." A century before, a criticism of Roman legions in battle would not have contained a reference to the condition of their bows. One can only suppose that, unofficially at least, the bow was becoming a weapon which ranked with the time-honored javelin in Roman estimation. Dio also notes that at the same time Varus was being cut to pieces in the Wald, one of his subordinates held the fortress of Aliso by manning the breastworks with legion archers.

Roman archery was almost entirely derivative, its main sources being Cretan, Grecian and latterly, Asiatic. Like the Greeks and probably following their practice, Roman archers drew the string to the chest, a rather ineffective method, at best. It was not until the reign of Emperor Maurice of

Byzantine that the draw was changed, by imperial edict, to the face for increased efficiency, and this was during the Later Roman Empire. Maurice also codified the use of archers in warfare and his concept of the value of archery can readily be seen in a surviving quotation, "We wish that every young Roman of free condition should learn the use of the bow and should be constantly provided with that weapon."

The bows used in the Roman army were mostly of the reflex form, since they were handled by men well used to this type of weapon. The largest single exception to this was in the case of the African mercenaries, who used the flat or longbows common to their country of origin. Since Rome was rich in metal, the arrowheads of her *auxilia* were iron or steel. The quiver was common to all their archers and bowstrings varied from people to people. One letter describes bowstrings made from the tendons of horses.

Among the later Roman emperors, we find several who prided themselves on their ability with the bow. Both Suetonius and Herodian report that Domitian and Commodus were expert archers, and Theodosius is sometimes said to have excelled in the sport. Gibbon, in his *Decline and Fall of the Roman Empire* says that the Emperor Gratian was rather overly impressed by the archery skill of the Alans. The Alans (Allands) were another of the nomad horse tribes who came into Europe from Asia and it is not surprising that they were good bowmen. Gratian learned the use of the bow from Alan instructors and although he himself never became highly proficient at the art, he copied the dress and arms of his Alan preceptors.

Domitian combined his target archery with a form of sadism, a quality not uncommon in the annals of imperial Rome. To amuse himself and his friends, Domitian had boy slaves placed some distance away and then would shoot arrows between the spread fingers of his targets. Fortunately the historians have spared us the details of the practice necessary to attain this singular degree of skill.

Commodus was even prouder of his skill as a marksman. In order that more people should appreciate his talents, he often took part in the great games. From the imperial box he is supposed to have killed one hundred lions with one hundred arrows. Obviously Commodus was gifted as a marksman and he is remembered for a new style of arrowhead, which he had forged. This extraordinary head was used by the emperor to shoot at running ostriches, which he decapitated with one arrow. The head was in the form of a half-moon, with the cutting edge, the concave arc. But the trick shot which pleased Commodus, and the people, the most was at big cats. A condemned criminal was tied to a stake in the center of the arena and one of the lions, tigers or leopards was let loose at the far side. The great cat, starved and ill-tempered, would almost immediately begin to creep up on his helpless victim. Then, just as the cat tensed for the killing leap, Commodus, clad in purple, would rise to his feet and speed an arrow to the animal's heart. As a variant the emperor sometimes shot from a sitting position.

While archery, as a sport, was becoming popular in Rome as a result of these imperial whims, in the army it was growing to be more and more the weapon. The legions themselves had become but shadows of their former selves and dependency was placed on mercenaries to a large extent. Many of these foreigners were from Asia, and they taught others their skills with the bow and arrows, so that by the time of the Emperor Justinian, almost all the Roman forces were skilled archers.

During Justinian's reign, the Roman general Belisarius undertook the reconquest of North Africa, which had fallen into the hands of the Goths. Although some historians make the Goths archers, most are agreed that they and the other Teutonic tribes were singularly inept with the bow. Procopius says, in his *Gothic Wars,* "And the difference was this, that practically all the Romans and their allies, the Huns, are good mounted bowmen but not a man among the Goths has had practice in this branch, for their horsemen are accustomed to use only spears and swords, while what few bowmen they have enter battle on foot and under cover of the heavily armed men. So the horsemen, unless the engagement is at close quarters, have no means of defending themselves against opponents who use the bow, and therefore can easily be reached by the arrows of the Romans and destroyed."

One Roman emperor died with a bow in his hands. He was Valentinian, ruler of the West, whose General Aetius defeated the Huns at the historic battle of Châlons. When Aetius returned to Rome he became involved in political intrigue and Valentinian, fearful of the general's popularity with the people, had him executed on false charges. Aetius seems to have been a man who commanded respect and loyalty, for two years after his death, two Huns who had been his personal attendants crept up behind the emperor while he was practicing archery outside Rome and strangled him as he loosed an arrow at the targets.

The Roman Empire had long since been divided into two halves—one ruled from Constantinople and the other, weaker half, from Rome itself. Although relations between the two halves were often strained, Constantinople did try to save her sister city on more than one occasion. From one of these expeditions we get a clear picture of the uses of archery in a hill campaign.

Narses, the Byzantine commander, was a eunuch—steeped in intrigue and deviousness—but he was at the same time an able tactician. He evolved a battle plan using archers which was to remain unparalleled until Edward III duplicated it inadvertently at Crécy. Narses arrived at Taginae in the foothills of the Apennines late in the year 552. His expedition was aimed at breaking the power of the Goths, who were at that time mercilessly ravaging the entire Italian peninsula.

The Gothic attack plan was simple. Heavy mounted cavalry charged straight for their objective and if they failed to take it in the first attempt, they reformed to try again, and again until they themselves were beaten, or the objective gained. Like many primitive tribes they depended on shock power for success instead of subtlety or finesse. Their bravery is unquestioned, but their tactical ability was of a very low level.

The two armies camped facing each other along the edge of the hills. Narses took the strategic advantage of placing the high ground to his rear, thereby interfering with the free maneuvering of the Gothic cavalry. Just before midafternoon he sent forward a party of fifty of his best bowmen to take and hold a small hill which commanded the Gothic camp. In spite of concentrated efforts, the Goths failed to dislodge the archers and they remained in their position all night, harrowing the cavalry camp with intermittent flights of arrows. At dawn Narses sent a runner forward, ordering them to retreat to the Roman lines.

The eunuch's position was designed to completely ward off the Gothic attack. At his center he had dismounted eight thousand heavy cavalry, or foederati, in a solid phalanx. On either wing and thrown forward were four thousand archers, who were protected by a force of five hundred cavalry on either side. The slope of the land gave an added advantage in that the archers were able to pour their fire slightly down, onto the open area in front of the phalanx.

The Goths, under their leader Totila, as usual, staked their success on the first charge, and barring that, on succeeding waves of heavy armed horsemen. They began by attacking directly at the center of the Roman line, completely disregarding the archers on either flank. Within the horns of Narses' lines, the slaughter was immediate and devastating.

Men and horses fell in great clumps and those riders who escaped wounding found their horses killed under them. Only the rear ranks of the Gothic lines escaped the carnage, but Totila seemingly failed to see the hopelessness of his tactics. In all the Goths made twelve successive charges into the arc of the Roman battle line, each time facing the swarms of arrows which brought death before the bearded, shouting warriors could close with the phalanx. Even scattered attempts by small bodies of Gothic horse to seize the archers' positions were repulsed by heavy, steady arrow fire and the day resulted in a total Roman victory.

Had Totila concentrated his heavy first attempts in an effort to turn the Roman flanks, Taginae might have had an entirely different result. But the positions of the archers in respect to the land would have crippled the Gothic chances of success and, secondly, Narses had been entirely correct in analyzing Gothic battle psychology. The successful use of bowmen in battle depended on the abilities of the individual commanders. In the hands of one, the bow became almost invincible; in the hands of another, the bow was a weak, hardly dependable weapon.

As the years passed, the center of the Roman empire came to reside exclusively in the east, and it was here that the Emperor Leo published a treatise on warfare. Although commonly accepted as his own work, the treatise is actually a rewrite of the earlier work issued by Maurice, in which, as we have seen, the draw of the bow was changed. Leo's work also ordered exact battle plans suitable for specific circumstances. An example is the order to form the heavy infantry as the front rank, with light-armed archer infantry as the second rank. As battle begins, the archers are to shoot over the heads of the front rank. This first stage is immediately followed by a charge of Byzantine cavalry. If the cavalry move proved successful in softening up the enemy's line, the infantry then advanced at the double, while the archers kept pace, laying down a barrage of arrow fire, to further disorder and disorganize the opposition.

These plans showed a shrewd appreciation of the need for coordination between missile and shock, or arrow fire and infantry contact. Leo's and Maurice's maxims were adhered to for centuries and it is a tribute to their efficiency that the Eastern Roman Empire continued for as long as it did, for its troops were largely mercenary and often rebellious or mutinous. Adherence to book precepts can, however, have the effect of robbing commanders of initiative and flexibility.

In 1071 came the actual downfall of Roman power at the battle of Manzikert. Here Byzantine troops, under Romanus and following the rules of their texts, met Turkish horse archers under the leadership of Alp Arslan. The Turks were overwhelmingly victorious and Constantinople never really recovered from the defeat. From that point on, until the absorption of the city into Turkish hands, the Byzantine empire depended on diplomacy and psychology—not on troops. The reason for the Turkish victory seems simple; although both Leo and Maurice had laid down tactics which could be used in battle with nomadic horsemen, they had not foreseen the tremendous concentration of Turks, nor the ability of their leaders. Alp Arslan was a first-rate cavalryman and his use of horse archers put an end to the infantry-archer-cavalry sequence of the Byzantines.

Roman archery, from first to last, was a weak thing. The bow never gained the popularity and strength which it deserved, particularly in the West. Roman successes during the time of the legions were overwhelming, but would they have been against great archers?

6

The Scourges of God—Archers Out of Asia

ALTHOUGH WE MUST, AND DO, PAY TRIBUTE TO THE BOWMEN of England and to the archery-woodscraft of the American Indian, we cannot escape the fact that archery reached its climax in Asia. Perhaps archery originated somewhere in this, the largest of the continents, and if it did not, the bow certainly came into use at a very early date there. Since then, Asia has truly been the land where there were "Kingdoms of the Bow." If those kingdoms did not last, did not become too great a part of world history, it is not because the bow failed as a weapon, but rather because of the nature of the men who wielded those bows.

Asia was for many centuries a continent shrouded in mystery. A combination of geography and politics served as a more than efficient cloak to keep the men of the western world from penetrating its secrets. It is only within the past one hundred years that we have begun to know what Asia is really like. Geography has in large part been overcome, in this search for the unknown, but unfortunately politics still contrive to keep much of Asia a matter of guesswork. Most of our knowledge of Asia then is peripheral, in more than one sense.

If this is true today, it is more than true of the past. Only when Asia and the Asiatics suddenly impinged on the consciousness of the Occident, did our ancestors really think about the subject. It was a *terra incognita,* fit to house the lands and creatures, the peoples and phantoms of the story tellers. Only when one of the periodic waves of people, moving out of the homelands, hit on the shores of Europe are there any real records. And these too are clouded by conjecture and tinged with what amounted to superstitious terror.

Herodotus wrote of the Scyths from pure hearsay and by that token we must make allowances for distortion. The Scyths were Asiatics but were they yellow or white? Where had they come from? Where did they go? Many authorities see in the Scyths of the Classic Greeks nothing more than the ancestors of the Huns, but this in an unprovable claim. Other men, equally learned, say that the Scyths were Iranian, therefore they were Caucasians and since the Huns were Mongoloid, and therefore yellow, the Huns and the Scyths could not possibly be the same people.

Whoever they were, the Huns formed the first of the great waves of archers to rise out of Central Asia and fall on Europe, to the consternation of church and state and the abject terror of the people. Perhaps we can find some traces of the Huns in early Chinese records.

Before the birth of Christ, a nation appeared to the north of what we know as China and laid waste to the land, in a typical nomadic style. They were called the Hiung-Nu, and it was said of them that their country was the back of a horse. They were incredibly tough, simple, barbarous and ambitious. They were only one tribe out of many who ranged the northern borders of the already old kingdom of China. Being ambitious, the Hiung-Nu found it far more expedient to work for the Chinese than to raid and harass them. They became the border guards, protecting their Chinese masters from the inroads of the other tribes around them. The situation, however, was one of constant flux where in one decade the Hiung-Nu might be steadfast in their trust while in the next they might raid deep into China. Even the Great Wall did not deter them when they made up their minds to ravage the soft countryside within.

Every able-bodied man of the tribe was a warrior. If he could draw a bow, he was a trooper. The children from infancy were trained as riders and archers and early visitors to their camps speak of seeing the Hiung-Nu children riding about among the tents on the backs of sheep, practicing with toy bows and arrows on the rats and vermin which infested the camp sites.

If the Hiung-Nu were not Iranian—that is, not Caucasian —they were certainly subject to a great many Iranian influences. For we find that the Sarmatians, who were probably closely related to the Alans, taking service with the Hiung-Nu along the Chinese borders. The Sarmatians were the precursors of the Middle Ages and like the Parthians, went into battle in full armor, with their horses equally well protected. What is more important is their introduction into Hiung-Nu territory of the triangular arrowhead. This form which is today almost universal, came originally from Iranian territory during the early Iron Age, and spread with Iranian cultural influences.

Another form of Iranian culture which penetrated into central Asia and northern China at an early date was the combination bow case and quiver which was typical of the western steppes. The case was called a *gorytus* and examples, in precious metals, have been unearthed from early Scythian burial mounds in the Caspian region. Whether or not the *gorytus* came to the Hiung-Nu from the Sarmatians, who used the bow as a secondary weapon, we do not know. But it is another example of the blending of cultures which occurred across Asia as early as the second century before Christ. When the Hiung-Nu eventually moved westward toward Europe they brought the *gorytus* with them, as did every succeeding wave to run over into the West.

Our knowledge of these Hiung-Nu is drawn exclusively from early Chinese records, and Orientalists are frank to admit that in many cases the Chinese writers were referring to these people from the same point of view Herodotus used in describing the Scyths, that of hearsay. It would be interesting to know how much truth there was to the report that the Hiung-Nu possessed equines which are unknown today. Were these sports, developing in those vast plains and deserts during the time man was taming the tarpan, and if so, why did they eventually die out? Or were the old Chinese having a bit of fun at the expense of their readers?

For a period of approximately four hundred years the Hiung-Nu continued their work as border guards and border raiders. Peace, in the commonly accepted sense, never existed along those borders. If no other tribes threatened the marches, the Hiung-Nu themselves would storm across the Wall and lay waste to the land, bringing home with them the wealth of cities and the women of nations. Sometimes they rode alone, sometimes with raiders from allied tribes, with whom they were temporarily at peace. All of these warriors, no matter what their tribe, were expert archers and perhaps the best riders in the world. They slept in the saddle, swore oaths on their arrows and drank the blood of their horses when other food was not available.

At one point a legendary king appears among the Hiung-Nu, called Meghder. Son of another Hiung-Nu chieftain, he had been given as a hostage by his father in some intertribal pact and barely escaped from his captivity with his life. For this he bore his father, T'ou-man, a grudge which seems to have tinged most of his life. Once more restored to his rights as the heir-apparent to the Hiung-Nu throne, he was given command of a large body of troops. Discipline among these tribes was almost nonexistent, warriors owing allegiance, not obedience, to the tribal chiefs. But Meghder was made of sterner stuff and he instilled into his men a sense of discipline. At the same time, so the story goes, he invented a whistling arrow, which the Chinese called *ming-ti* and the Japanese knew as *nari-kabura*. Such arrows were common in almost every culture which used the bow, the usual form being a head which was pierced with holes parallel to the axis of the shaft. As the arrow sped through the air, pressure set up by the spinning of the shaft set up a whistling. Such arrows were used for a variety of purposes, some to carry messages over city walls, but in the main they were used as a signal.

This was Meghder's purpose and he trained his disciplined troops to shoot at any target which he indicated with his whistling shafts. His training was such that finally his men shot automatically—some accounts describe him executing troopers who failed in a series of tests. When the men were trained to perfection, Meghder took them with him on a royal hunt. When his father, T'ou-man, advanced in front of the prince, the young regicide shot him with the whistling arrow and in an instant the king fell, "and so full was his body with arrows that he could not lie upon the ground."

Meghder was apparently an able administrator, for later in his career we find that he wrote to his overlord, the Han Emperor Wen-Ti, and told him that the border was finally at peace, "for I have welded all those nations who use the bow from horseback into one kingdom under my command."

Periodically the Chinese attempted to plant colonies north of the Great Wall and in so doing encroached on the grazing lands of the tribes. This too brought conflict between the Chinese and the Hiung-Nu, since the nomads considered their rights to the grass lands as inalienable. Meghder's son, Zengi Kayuk fought long and hard against one of these periodic waves of Chinese expansion. Finally after long wars with the Chinese he won the concession that all north of the Great Wall was to be the land of the bowmen and all that lay south (in China itself) was to be the "land of hats and girdles." This somewhat picturesque phrase must not, however, be taken to mean that the Chinese themselves were not archers, for through centuries of contact with the horse archers of the north, they themselves had become skilled with the bow.

The ravagings of the Hiung-Nu finally drove the Chinese to the breaking point, and with the help of other nomad tribes, they chased their border guards away from the area of their sinecure. The Hiung-Nu moved north and west, leaving a spatial vacuum at the top of China which was almost immediately filled by another tribe of nomadic archers, the Sien-pi. This was a branch of the great Tungus group, which was to figure largely in the later history of the Mongols. The Sien-pi came into the space left by the Hiung-Nu, from the northeast and many of their bows were made from the horns of the musk ox. Since horn must be worked in the form of a composite bow, we can assume that the Sien-pi were already well advanced in the art of bowyery. Horn will not function in the form of a self-bow but must be cut and fitted with some degree of nicety, to be used in conjunction with other materials to make a good bow.

It is logical to assume that a composite bow, in the short reflex form, developed as the result of two primary causes. One is, of course, the lack of suitable materials to make self-bows. This would be especially true of the semiarid regions of Mid-Asia, where the growth of any type of wood is stunted by nature. The second factor is the ease of handling the short bow as compared with a longbow. There are a few isolated instances where horsemen used a longbow, but they are the exceptions which prove the rule, for by and large, horse archers favor a short, heavily reflexed bow, which gives maximum cast, maximum penetration and optimum maneuverability in the saddle.

The Sien-pi, having come from the north, as evidenced by their use of musk-ox horn, did not come from a land barren of workable timber. The Siberian tundra is still covered with trees and although they may not be among the best bow woods in the world, some of them certainly would be usable. Even poor bow woods can be reinforced and strengthened with sinew, for use in the saddle—a fact which North American tribes exploited fully. Therefore we come to the conclusion that the Sien-pi bows were composite on the basis of their use as horse-borne weapons, and that the tribal craft was far enough advanced so that the bowyers appreciated and could utilize the superior cast of horn.

In the meantime the displaced Hiung-Nu moved on. If they themselves had created a vacuum when they moved, they did not find a place for their herds and tents but instead, other tribes of equally barbaric clansmen, well entrenched and prepared to defend their holdings. The Hiung-Nu road was a constant way of battle—for space, for grazing, for water. Here and there they succeeded in temporarily displacing some smaller tribe, and in spots they dropped off contingents of their own clans, who found new territory to their liking.

One such group were called Turks by the Chinese. They are not to be confused with the later Turks, the Osmanli and Seljuks. These were instead people known as the Western Turks, who finally disappeared from history, probably founding or being absorbed into the Kankali, or the People of the High Carts. The Western Turks were only a small branch of the main body of the Hiung-Nu, but in their prime they were not a little tribe. Under their leader, Mer-co they possessed a standing army of four hundred thousand horse archers, ever ready to raid and pillage or to defend the tribal grazing grounds. As the tribe became more firmly established in the land they were broken into ten subtribes, called the Ten Arrows. The partition was so named from the Arrows of Authority, presented to each chieftain as a symbol of his office. The Arrows could be recalled if the paramount chieftain felt that his subordinates were at fault in their ruling. War was signaled by a call being issued for the Ten Arrows to assemble, in the quiver of the tribe.

The symbolism of archery has been in the past worldwide, particularly among more primitive peoples, but nowhere was it as common as in Asia. In addition to the Ten Arrows of the Turks, they also utilized a levy system, with arrowheads as the mark of authority. When they wished to raise a certain number of cattle or sheep from their subjects, the chief would inscribe the number wanted on a piece of wood or ivory and, as the seal of his authority, an arrowhead was fixed after the number. The arrowhead continued to be the mark of authority until as late as the year 1875, when the arrow was the death warrant issued by the Manchu dynasty in China. Under the Mongol emperors, after Genghis Khan, the bow itself symbolized the king or supreme ruler, and the arrow was the symbol of the ambassador, the representative of that rule.

In the great Indian epic the Mahabharata, archery is often mentioned, and there is one rather pretty tale about the hero, Arjuna, using a symbolically strong bow. These terrifically heavy bows are universal, the ability to use them being considered proof of semidivinity. The Hindu tale also postulates the princess who can only be won by use of the bow.

Arjuna travels to the country of the Panchalas because he has heard great tales concerning the beauty of Draupadi, the daughter of the king. Arriving he finds that her hand can only be won by an archer. The test requires the suitor to string a great bow and then to shoot five arrows in succession through a spinning wheel, beyond which lies the target. If the suitor hits the target with all five arrows he will receive the hand of the princess, but should he fail in any part of the test, his life is forfeit. Arjuna disguises himself and essays the test. Because of his semidivinity he is of course successful, and claiming his bride prize, he takes Draupadi off with him to be wife to himself and to his four brothers.

Because the bow and the horse formed the natural basis for the nomadic life, it is not strange that both should play such a large part in the symbolic life of these peoples, and we can suppose that the archer Arjuna represents a throwback in time to an era when archery played a large part in

Indian life. Since Aryan conquerors in India originally came from the steppe country, it would seem that they had preserved at least certain traditions similar to those still used to the north.

As the Scythians had used the arrow in a ceremony to seal a pact, so the Kalmucks swore an oath and, licking the head of an arrow, plunged it into the ground with the head pointing to the sky. The religion of these barbarians was simple and in it the everyday things of their lives played a large part. The Kankalis, for example, believed in thunder as the harbinger of good grazing, and when a thunderstorm was anywhere near, the warriors of the tribe rode at full speed to be in the heart of the storm. At the storm center they shouted up at the sky, at the same time shooting as many arrows as possible toward the clouds. Then they rode back to their camp and moved immediately. The following year they returned, sure that the area would have been made fertile and rich by this offering of arrows to the storm gods.

In some cases, this preoccupation with archery from a religious standpoint carried over into the nomadic concept of the afterlife. The right hand of the warrior was the hand which held the bowstring. The bowstring was all important, and by extension the right hand must be signally honored after death. Thus in certain tribes, if the khan or chieftain died, it was customary for the princelings and nobles who had served him to approach the body in turn, while each man shot an arrow into the right hand of the corpse.

We have previously mentioned the burials around Lake Baikal, where the dead were equipped with bows and arrows. Weapon burial is of course not new—it ranged from the Stone Age to the time of the early West, where men were buried with their "six-guns"—but some steppe tribes made weapon burial realistic. The Kankalis, the "thunder worshipers," buried their dead in a sitting position and did not cover the grave, but rather left it open to both time and scavengers. In the hands of the deceased they placed a strung and drawn bow, the string pulled back and held in position behind cunningly made braces which were hidden behind the nocked and ready arrow.

Other tribes were even more practical in their use of the bow to protect the dead. As some of the chieftains became wealthy, through raiding and war, they found that it was sometimes difficult to guard the treasures in the graves. Pilfering from tombs was, and is, a time-honored custom the world over. To guard against grave robbers, the Mongols developed elaborate mantraps, which used bows as the killing agents. Unfortunately, an accurate description of their workings is lost, but we do have a quote on the subject from the Abbé Huc, who spent years in Central Asia:

"To protect the treasures they place in the cavern a kind of bow, capable of discharging a number of arrows, one after the other. This bow (or rather several bows joined together) are already bent and the arrows ready to fly. They place the machine so that on opening the door of the cavern, the movement causes the discharge of the first arrow at the man or men who enter. The discharge of the second follows and so on to the last."

The Hiung-Nu continued to move to the west and eventually found themselves on the extreme edge of the Eastern Roman Empire. Here they adapted their old tactics and hired themselves out as border guards to the Byzantines. With one hand they accepted the gold of their "overlords" and with the other they raided deep into their territory. In front of them, smaller tribes fled in haste and the whole of the Near East and Europe was thrown into a state of turmoil by the advance of the Hiung-Nu, known now as the Huns.

History tells in full the story of Attila, the Hun, called "The Scourge of God." Chronicles, tales and legend are full of the terror which beset men when the name of the Hun chief was mentioned, and his memory is perpetuated in the evil dwarf Alberich of the Nibelunglied. Actually, Attila

was a highly successful cavalryman, with a flair for administration. In addition to the men of his own tribe he mustered
in his ranks warriors from among the Herules, the Gepids,
the Scyri, the Lombards, the Rugians, the Goths and a
dozen other nations now lost in time. This was the horde
which swept unchecked into Europe, stopping only after
the decisive battle of Châlons.

Despite Attila's abilities as a campaigner and organizer,
he lacked an adequate knowledge of logistics, the supplying
of troops in the field. The Hunnish policy of turning all land
into pasturage was not designed to feed and equip an army
on the march, nor were all of Attila's allies as capable of
fending for themselves in the field. In consequence his was
not an army but a mounted rabble of horsemen, most of
them archers, living off the land and unable to turn back—
they left no living thing behind them. Bold, brave and cunning the Huns certainly were, but they were hit-and-run fighters, completely unfitted psychologically for long campaigns
or sieges.

The Huns were content to face their enemy and sit the
saddle discharging clouds of arrows, at the same time utter-
ing uncouth war cries. Then and then only, when the resistance of the enemy had been broken by the tremendously
heavy missile fire, did the Huns risk body contact. These
tactics were admirably suited for warfare on the steppes,
against similar tribes. They were, moreover, suited against
foot soldiery, but they needed at all times an element of
cohesiveness. Attila supplied that, and the Hunnish dominions were boundless as long as Attila lived. With his death
the power of the Huns vanished and they crept back to the
steppes, to disappear from history, save for the name Hungary.

At Châlons, Attila faced a desperate, last-stand army under
Aetius, the Roman, and Theodoric, the Goth. Driven by
danger to fight together, these two put into the field an army
which was almost as formidable as that of Attila. And like

the Hun general's force, the Romano-Gothic troops were also, for the most part, light-armored, heavy-bowed cavalry. At the historic battle, then, the decision hinged on hard fighting and discipline. Both sides were similarly equipped and used essentially similar tactics, for many of Aetius' men had trained under, or in some instances, were commanded by Huns. Both sides carried reserves of arrows so that throughout the fight, flight after flight of shafts flew from side to side. In the end, the superior discipline of the Roman lead troops gave them the initiative. Held in position by the Romano-Gothic missile fire, the Huns suffered when Theodoric rode into their lines with bodies of heavy armed Gothic cavalry, which crushed the nomads.

Although Châlons is counted as one of the great victories of the West, considerable mystery surrounds its outcome. True, Attila had been very hard pressed at the end of the day's fighting, but it was not an outright victory—the Huns still had sufficient men to continue the battle. Neither Aetius nor Theodoric followed up their slight advantage, however, and Attila was allowed to withdraw into a fortress of wagons and tents. There the nomads and their allies spent the night, repelling several small stabbing feints by the Roman troops. On the following day the Huns retreated, without interference from Aetius.

The retirement was temporary and within a comparatively short time the Huns were racing down the Italian peninsula, intent on capturing Rome. Almost total disorganization set in among the Roman forces, and the retreat of the Huns from this campaign was due, to Roman arms and valor, but to the fact that again Attila was living off the land and supplies ran short, while disease riddled the ranks of his men. The salvation of the city of Rome was what amounted to a miracle, but Italy for centuries bore the scars of the invasion. Even prayers in the Italian churches reflected the fear which struck into the souls of all men. This was the terror which inspired the prayer, *"A sagittarii Hunorum, nos defenda,*

Domine"—"From the arrows of the Huns, O Lord, defend us."

While the Huns depended on their tremendous rate of missile fire for the majority of their victories, they were, as well, fully aware of the value of psychological warfare. Their appearance was, by all accounts, repulsive and terrifying and they did nothing to change it, knowing that if their names and faces brought fear to their opponents, half their battles were won. Even Châlons was a measure of desperation and would probably never have been fought except for the fact that all of Europe and its nascent Christianity had its back to the wall. In the instance of the actual invasion of Italy, nothing military stemmed the Hunnish tides—noble and churchman, farmer and soldier alike fled before the nomads. The few cities in their path were left alone, for Attila realized the impotence of his horde in siege warfare. When he died, the first great wave of horse archers ceased to influence Europe. Only in the tales and histories did any memory of these men remain, and they did nothing to prepare the West for the waves which were to follow in later centuries. Attila had been the Anti-Christ, and his men the demons of hell, appearing out of unknown Asia. With the passing of the Huns, Central Asia ceased to exist in European minds.

In China the bow continued to be part of everyday life. When a child was born into a house, it was customary to hang a bow and a quiver of arrows at the door, if the child was a boy. Even the gentle philosopher Confucius spoke of archery, although one does not expect him to treat of such a warlike subject. In his Book of Sentences, Confucius says, "By the drawing of the bow, one can know the virtue and conduct of men." Archery was treated by the Chinese with that same respect and ritual which they awarded to so many things. Each sport must be conducted along certain definite lines, and to break these rules was a most arrogant breach of "face." To the Chinese, archery was not only a powerful arm, deadly in war and the chase, but it occupied an honored place in their roster of relaxations. In another passage Confucius gives us a list of the distances at which various classes were to shoot and also a list of the targets assigned to each section of society. An emperor was to shoot from a distance of 120 yards and his target was to be a bearskin, a king shot for eighty yards at the hide of a stag, while a mandarin used a tiger skin as target from seventy yards. Last came the men of letters, who shot at fifty yards, using a boarskin as a mark. It is interesting that none of these marks would prove difficult to the average modern archer, so that we can safely assume the standard of target shooting in Confucius' time to have been considerably lower than our own.

But target shooting and war were not the only uses for the bow. Much of China was then wild country with a great deal of game. While India is traditionally the home of the tiger, in fact the animal occurred throughout much of western Asia. In the section of China now known as Yunnan, many of the great striped cats roamed, and there are records of tiger hunting there with bows and dogs. The most readable of the accounts is that of Marco Polo, the first great Asiatic explorer. What the dogs were which he mentions in this story we cannot say, unless they were related to the extremely fierce and vicious Tibetan mastiffs.

"In this country are likewise found the largest and fiercest dogs that can be met with anywhere—so courageous and powerful are they, that a man with a couple of them may be more than a match for a tiger. Armed with a bow and arrows and thus attended, should he meet with a tiger, he sets on his intrepid dogs, who instantly advance and attack the tiger. The animal instinctively seeks shelter against a tree, so as to place himself in order that the dogs may not be able to get behind him and that he may have his enemies in front. With this as his intention as soon as he perceives the dogs, he makes his way toward the tree, but with a very slow pace, and by no means at a run, so that he may not show any sign of fear, which the pride of the animal would not allow.

"During this deliberate movement, the dogs fasten upon him and the man plies him with arrows. He, in his turn, endeavors to seize the dogs, but they are too nimble for him and draw back, when he resumes his slow march, but before he can gain his position he has been wounded by so many arrows, and so often bitten by the dogs, that he falls through weakness and from loss of blood. By these means it is that he is at length taken."

One does not like to question Marco Polo, for he was so often correct in his stories, but it is difficult to see how an archer would have been able to kill a tiger by these means. Most modern experience tends to prove that the tiger is all too ready to meet attack with attack. Even if the cat did slink away in the face of the dogs, it would have been necessary for the archer actually to tree the tiger before he could shoot at his target—without endangering the lives of his dogs. That it is possible to kill the big cats with a bow has been amply and ably illustrated by Saxton Pope and Art Young in Africa, and more recently by Howard Hill, in the course of a well-documented safari. A well-placed shaft from a heavy bow should be fatal to a tiger but if "he has been wounded by so many arrows," we begin to see either very light bows or very ineffectual arrows. No doubt the natives of Yunnan killed tigers with a bow and using dogs, but the Polo narrative does not seem to tell all the story.

Marco Polo's Yunnan tigers can be classed with the female gazelle shot by the Shah Ghazan of Persia, before some two thousand witnesses. The royal huntsman was using a peculiar arrowhead which the Mongols called "tuin." It was distinguished by having three points in one, so that its striking area somewhat resembled a trident. When the shah loosed his arrow, it seemed to the assembled hunters that he had missed because the animal was in midleap. Suddenly the quarry fell to the ground in a heap and when the shah galloped up it was found that he had shot it while springing in the air with its four feet together, all of which were wounded. Wounds also had been made in its flank, belly, breast, neck and throat, making altogether nine wounds. This wonderful shot was deemed thereafter to have excelled that of the famous Persian hero Bahram-gur, who was reported to have hit a wild ass when in the air, pinning its hoof to its ear with his arrows. In both instances we are faced with the fact that the Asiatics were either prodigious archers or prodigious liars and perhaps both.

War, however, was the principal field for archery throughout Asiatic history. In order fully to understand the part which the bow played in these pages, we must stop to analyze certain aspects of the Oriental character in relation to shock and missile tactics.

If two men fight, unarmored and hand-to-hand, the combat is pure shock. But if one of the men stands off and throws rocks at his opponent, he is using missile tactics. Any variation or amplification of this can be reduced back to its simplest elements. Therefore, any use of the bow in warfare, defensive or offensive, introduced the missile element. The factors of protection—in the form of armor or of walls; the factors of mobility—on foot, on horseback, or in airplanes, are in effect "extra added attractions" which embroider the basic pattern of shock and missile.

We can see in the development of medieval warfare in Europe that shock was the element on which most military leaders based their campaigns. The missile warfare of the English bowmen and the Swiss crossbowmen were the exceptions which proved the rule. Radically opposed to this viewpoint, Oriental practice depended, in the main, on missiles. Certainly shock was never completely absent—in fact it never can be in war, but it was not the deciding factor. Psychologists might be able to explain this, but outstanding in all the annals of Oriental warfare is the readily apparent dislike of physical contact which characterizes their battles. In daily life this same abhorrence of "physicalization" tinges Oriental thinking and behavior patterns so that it actually is not surprising to find it carried over into the field. One can carry this assumption one stage further and postulate the theory that Oriental conquerors were unwilling to come to grips with their opponents, even on a mental level, and that therefore their conquests were fleeting—for we find that their conquests rarely lasted beyond the lifetime of the individual leader, except in those cases where the conquests represented the imposition of Oriental thought on Oriental thought.

Another strong factor in the breakdown of these empires was that during their periods of maximal expansion, they usually depended on the organizational and administrative genius of one man, rather than on a dynasty. These qualities, so essential to leadership, were not universally distributed but rather occurred only occasionally and in rare instances. Between them and the average warrior there was no middle class of men, capable of assuming the tasks of coordination. We have already witnessed the rapid disintegration of the Hunnish empire on the death of Attila, and we see much the same pattern repeated by the heirs of Genghis Khan and Tamerlane. If in the latter instances there were huge segments of the empire which continued, we must remember that they were just segments—not the whole. Had the sons of these men possessed the qualities of the fathers in full measure, today's history would have to be rewritten. Even though they did not, we must take the successes of the sires into consideration whenever we seek to understand the Oriental mind.

Genghis Khan was almost unquestionably the greatest cavalry commander the world has ever known. As a young man he was landless and hunted, the dispossessed heir of a petty tribal chieftain in Mid-Asia. As an old man he was an emperor, ruling from the Arctic Ocean to the Red Sea and from

the Sea of China to the Volga River. No single man in recorded history has held such vast dominions and been the
overlord of so many races. Genghis Khan was the terror of
his world and to him men gave the same name they had
given to Attila, "The Scourge of God." His reputation has
been that of a ruthless sadist, specializing in callous, unwar-
ranted brutality. Many even go so far as to attribute to him
the questionable distinction of first practicing genocide.

Yet before a wholesale condemnation of the man is issued
we should take into consideration the land from which he
sprang, the times in which he lived and the temper of his
race.

His real name was Temujin. His people were pastoral
herders and raiders. Their traditions, their thinking, their
lives and their hopes were based on the acquisition of great
flocks and herds. Water and grass were necessary to them—
pasturage and waterholes the objects of brief, bloody and
cruel intertribal wars. These Mongols were not simple,
peaceful herdsmen. There was never enough grass, and there
was never enough water for peace. Like the Huns before
them and the Turks after them, they rode from infancy and
the bow was never far from their hands. In periods of plenty
they gorged themselves on game that had fallen to their
arrows, and in lean times they existed on dried and
fermented milk. They had no real cities and few settlements.
Into their lives came Chinese traders with luxuries to offer
for the produce of the flocks. Soft fabrics and gaudy jewelry
gave them a glimpse of the richer world below the Great
Wall. Their own land was harsh and cruel, and they became,
of necessity, cruel and harsh. In the winter, winds whipped
for thousands of miles across the barrenness, driving bits of
snow and sand. In summer the winds blew only sand, and
heat rose in dancing waves or formed mirages to trap the soft,
unwary ones.

Life was cheap—children died in the cradle and men died
in the saddle, at the hands of their neighbors—but there was

never enough of anything to make life simple. One thing and one thing only the men of the steppes understood and that was the rule of strength. The death of weaklings and fools came either by the instrumentality of men or through the forces of nature—it made no difference. Even blood ties weakened in the face of strength—Temujin's uncles hunted him when he was landless, as viciously as though he had been a wolf.

The men called themselves "The Sons of the Wolf" and so Temujin became the Wolf of Wolves, the Khan of Khans, the Lord of the World. Through treachery and bravery, through cunning and skill, through strength and an innate sense of psychology, the great Mongol began to forge his kingdom. He was as implacable and cold as the land from which he came. His temper was hotter than the summer winds scorching across the great Gobi Desert, but he trained it and channeled it with cold harshness, like the snows of the Karakorum.

Men from a hundred tribes rallied to his banners, and when these horse archers moved, their arrows and the hoofs of their horses destroyed politics and geography alike. Cities vanished, and nations ceased to exist. Imperial China, proud and old, guarded by the Great Wall, became a Mongol fief, and the people of Kharesmia fled from their lands and found refuge in Egypt.

The secret of the Mongol success lay in what was literally overwhelming arrow fire. Genghis Khan, realizing the potential of Central Asia, channeled it through discipline and organization into an army. His was no unruly mob, but a vast military machine. Each warrior was armed and armored. Each warrior carried sixty arrows into battle. When a hundred thousand of the men of Genghis Khan rode into battle, no living force could oppose them for long.

Siege warfare was totally foreign to this mass of horse archers, a fact which Temujin took into consideration. His campaigning usually called for the horde to sweep past a city entirely, leaving it alone but taking good care to completely devastate the countryside around so that the people within the walls had no hope of replenishing their supplies. After the mass of men had moved by, he would suddenly detach perhaps ten thousand troopers, who would sweep back and, taking the city by complete surprise, succeed in capturing the defenses. Even if the sudden return was not a success, the troops would range the countryside, keeping the city penned in and eliminating any chance of reinforcements being brought up. It was only after the Mongol Empire was well formed that Temujin was able actually to invest and capture any large cities. Being wise, he incorporated in the army large numbers of Chinese engineers, who were well versed in the use of battering rams, mining, siege towers and explosives, along with every other form of siege equipment. It must be remembered that Genghis Khan took not only plunder but ideas—any ideas which were a means to his end. Since the average Mongol could neither read nor write, scribes from the many subject nations served the Khan. The Mongols had no real monetary system; coinage was introduced. As more and more provinces came under Mongol control they were ruled with a hand of iron, but with efficient soldier police, good highways, rapid courier service, freedom of religion, safe conduct for merchants and a system of rough justice for every man, and a hundred other amenities which had not existed prior to the rule of the Khan.

Like Attila before him, Genghis Khan was an astute psychologist. When survivors, fleeing before the Horde, brought word of their savagery, cities had a habit of opening their gates before it was necessary to bring up the Chinese with their siege engines. Genghis Khan was no open-handed, indolent potentate, but he paid well for services performed and knew the value of planting his own men within cities, to spread sedition and dissension. His discipline, based on reward and punishment, enabled him to rule without fear, even among so many subject nations. Once a city or a nation had submitted to him, he guarded it as fiercely as his own tribes.

The average Mongol, the trooper under the yak-tail banners of the Khan, was a happy man. Trained and toughened from infancy, he loved to fight, loved to ride, loved to loot, as long as he and his companions were successful. Their fanatical devotion to the Khan would not have stood up under any lengthy series of defeats.

This archer of the steppes, this "G.I. Joe" of the Kha Khan was short and stocky, with legs bowed from constant riding. His hair was short and black and straight, cropped closely and often left in a scalp lock, with the rest of the head bare. Loathing washing, he coated his body with grease to keep the cold out and the "essential humors" of the body in. His home was a felt tent called a yurta, which could be rolled up, off its frame of saplings, and was easily transported. Accustomed from childhood to the saddle, he would ride a horse a hundred yards in preference to walking. Rough, tanned sheepskin formed the bulk of his clothing, with fox and wolf fur for decoration. Winter and summer his feet were shod with felt boots, made during the long winter by the women of his home. Some of the tribes rode with their right shoulders bare, using the front of their jackets as capacious pouches, just as the Tibetans do today.

In war he wore armor of heavy lacquered leather, in the form of breast- and backplates, with a helmet. For arms he carried the ever-present bow and quiver, plus a small iron-shod mace, or in some instances a short stabbing lance. His shield was made of leather, round and stretched tight over a wooden frame, studded with copper or bronze and lacquered time and again. On the move his entire kit weighed less than twenty pounds and consisted mainly of dried milk, which he softened with water and carried under his saddle during the day's ride. When that ran short he was quite capable of dismounting and drinking the blood of his horse, by opening a vein in its leg, although he never endangered the health of his mount. A man on foot was an easy target. So inured was he to riding that he was capable of sleeping in the saddle while his horse grazed along the trail. His bowed legs came high on the sides of the horse, his stirrups were short so that when he shot his bow he stood upright in the saddle.

Among so many people from so many tribes, the bow was the paramount weapon, yet unfortunately we have few records to tell us the source of their arms. If at its peak the forces of the Great Khan numbered over five hundred thousand mounted bowmen, we are forced to one of two conclusions. Either there existed a tremendous number of bowyers and fletchers to equip this mass—and we find no record of such—or each trooper was himself able to make the reflexed composite bow and the various shafts which were in his normal kit. The majority of the information we have about the Mongols comes from the pens of their enemies or their subjects and for that reason is seldom subjective. Some few records are extant in the now rare Mongolian script, but almost no one has troubled to try to translate them into an Occidental language. Therefore, barring proof positive to the contrary, it is reasonable to assume that every man was his own bow maker and arrow maker, with perhaps the majority of the burden resting on the shoulders of the men who were too old to fight, who spent their days tending the flocks and their nights in making new bows and arrows for the warriors. It is true that in Mogul or Mongol India there existed a caste of bowyers, but this was the direct result of the religiously inspired compartmentation of living in the subcontinent, rather than a direct Mongol inheritance.

The bows were, as we have said, heavily reflexed, so as to obtain the maximum cast, without sacrificing any maneuverability while riding. Their makeup varied from tribe to tribe and from district to district, with the one rule that the bows were made from those materials which were most suitable to the area. Horn, sinew and wood were the basic components, blended in a variety of combinations. Modern bows from the same areas tend to make us believe that the maximum draw of the Mongol bow was seldom over one hundred pounds, in spite of the legends to the contrary. And this is a reasonable assumption, since it is seldom necessary to have heavier bows than that. If the need actually arose, there were probably special bows for special uses in the equipment trains of the army.

Insofar as arrows were concerned, however, the hordesman carried a variety of shafts, for diversified usage. Going into battle with sixty arrows, the ordinary trooper carried at least two main types. Thirty were light for long-distance shooting and the remainder were heavier, designed for armor piercing at shorter ranges. The shafts were universally of wood and made from trees similar to our beech. There were practice heads of horn, some made like Meghder's with holes so that their flight could be followed by ear. The "tuin" was reserved mostly for hunting, but for battle there were odd heads shaped like half-moons. Sometimes called the "eyebrow head," they were used for piercing the breastplates of the enemy. There was also a head made like the opened blades of a pair of scissors and designed specifically to cut off an opponent's arm at the shoulder joint. All these different types of arrows were carried in one quiver, which was compartmented to avoid mixing the shafts.

Because the Mongols were trained in archery almost before they could walk, we assume that the standard of their marksmanship was very high. Hunting was a national pastime with the tribesmen, and they guarded their flocks with the bow so that they must have been, at the very least, accurate. But the success of the Horde was not based on the individual and his abilities, but rather on the unit of individuals—which offered the advantages of mass discipline over the valor, courage and accuracy of the single warrior.

The entire Mongol force was based on a system of tens, so that a commander could order ten men, a hundred men or a thousand with equal facility. Because they carried their own meager supplies, the striking forces were independent of the land. Each year the warriors rode out from the home pasturages to follow the banners of the Horde and left the tending of the flocks and herds to the older people, to the women and to the children. At the start of a fresh campaign or a new season's fighting there were always thousands of young recruits from among the youths who had been herders before, so that the Horde never suffered from a lack of men. As the empire of Genghis Khan gained impetus he found tribe after tribe swarming to take service under his banners from the length and breadth of Inner Asia.

With limitless forces, vastly superior missile power and almost limitless mobility, Genghis Khan came closer than any other one man to completely conquering the world. Had he himself survived, the conquests would have continued—for all of Europe lay open to the advance of his men when the great Khan died. But internal strife and partition put an end to the vast dominions of Temujin and instead various kingdoms sprang up, ruled by his heirs and their various hordes. Genghis Khan was a man of great wisdom, and astute psychologist who realized all too well the shortcomings of his people. Although as the old tales related, "the grass went brown when the bowmen of the Great Khan rode by," the dissolution of empire was inevitable. Civilization softened the Horde, and to paraphrase Temujin himself, "they forgot the life which was the origin of their riches, forgot the stern somber necessity of the steppes. And when the time came, they lost all that he had won for them and given to them, and they were thrown back into the desert and the mountains where he found them, to wait and wait for a new leader."

One of the segments of Genghis Khan's empire which remained intact for a long period was in China. It was to the court of this kingdom that the Venetian traveler Marco Polo came with his father and his uncle, and it is from his account of the trip and the years he spent in the service of its Khan, Kublai, that we get our most vivid picture of Mongol life. It must be borne in mind that Kublai Khan was not a hard-riding Mongol but, removed by three generations from the steppes, he had taken on a heavy patina of Sino-culture. The memory of his grandfather Temujin was still green, but the "pleasure domes" of Peiping had already softened the men of the steppes. However, no account of Asiatic archery can be even partially complete without referring to Marco Polo's tale, and we find him saying of the Mongols, "no people on earth can surpass them in fortitude under difficulties nor show greater patience under wants of every kind."

Although the seat of Mongol rule had been transferred from Karakorum to Peiping, fresh levies of hard-riding troops always remained at the command of the emperor—raised in the traditional way from among the deserts and steppes and mountains. Of their fighting tactics, Polo remarks that they kept bodies of scouts two days in advance of their main body and also surrounded themselves with flankers and a strong rear guard and "when these Tartars (his generic name for the peoples of Central Asia) come to engage in actual battle, never do they mix directly with their enemies, but keep hovering about his sides, discharging their arrows from one side and then from the other. And on occasion they pretend to flee; during their flight they shoot arrows backward at their pursuers, thereby killing many men and horses, as though they were in combat, face to face. In this manner of making war the opponent comes to imagine that he is gaining a victory, when in actual fact he has lost the battle, for the Tartars, observing the havoc they have done him, wheel suddenly about and, renewing the fight, overpower the remainder of the enemy's troops."

During the period of Marco Polo's Chinese residence he was in service under the Khan, and he reports a great battle fought between the forces of the emperor and a rebellious chieftain named Nayan Khan. Most authorities agree that

Marco Polo was present at this battle and it represents, in this case, an eyewitness report of the fighting.

"Kublai took up his station in a great wooden castle, carried on the backs of four elephants, whose bodies were protected with coverings made of thick leather which had been hardened by fire and lacquer, over which were panels of cloth-of-gold. The castle contained, beside the emperor, many archers and crossbowmen, and on top of the castle was carried the imperial standard, which is an ornate representation of the sun and moon.

"His army, which consisted of thirty battalions of horse, each battalion containing ten thousand men armed with bows, the emperor placed in three grand divisions of ten battalions each: and those which formed the left and right wings he extended in such a manner as to outflank the wings of the army of Nayan. In front of each battalion of horse was posted a body of five hundred infantry, armed with short lances and swords, who, whenever the cavalry made a show of flight, were practiced to mount behind the riders and accompany them, alighting again when they returned to the charge and killing with their lances the horses and men of the enemy.

"As soon as the order of battle had been set, a tremendous number of wind instruments of various kinds were sounded, and these were followed by songs of a martial character, according to the custom of these Tartars before they began to fight. The commencement of battle is signaled by the cymbals and drums, and there was such a beating of the cymbals and drums and such singing, that it was altogether wonderful to hear.

"This signal to begin was given by the orders of the great Khan first to the wings and then to the center, and then a fierce and bloody conflict began. The air was instantly filled with a great cloud of arrows which poured down around on every side and huge numbers of men and horses were to be seen falling to the ground. The loud cries and shouts of the men, along with the noise of the horses and the sound of the bowstrings, were such as to inspire terror in the minds of those who heard them. When at last their arrows had been all discharged, the two armies met in close combat with their lances, swords and iron-shod maces and so great was the slaughter and so high were the heaps of the bodies of men and more especially of the horses, on the field, that it finally became impossible for one party to advance upon the other."

When the clans were not engaged in warfare or the guarding of their flocks and herds, they often took part in great hunts. They served a double purpose, for they not only supplied meat to entire tribes, but in their practice kept the riders fit for the rigors of war. Often they were held during the period of the *kuraltai*, when the clans and tribes were assembled to pay their annual homage to the great Khans and to transact the intertribal business of the empire. Then a messenger would pass from camp to camp, with word of the approaching hunt.

On the day appointed for the start, perhaps some twenty thousand men would assemble to take part. Stretching in a great circle, they gradually worked inward, constantly tightening their ranks. Sometimes the area surrounded would be half as big as the state of Texas and the hunt went on for a matter of weeks.

As the circle gradually grew smaller, the game which had been driven inward began to break from cover and the men would ride after it at full gallop, shrilling weird cries and discharging their arrows at the fleeing animals. Stationed at intervals along the rim of the riders were parties of nobles with falcons at their sides and when birds flushed at the horses' hoofs, the falcons were cast off to follow their prey high into the blue of the sky.

But the main purpose of the exercise was hunting with the bow. When the circle was at its smallest dimension, with the riders moving shoulder to shoulder, trumpets blared and the whole line stopped in position. Then into the open area, now full of game of every sort, rode the young warriors to show off their prowess with bow and horse. Certain kinds of game were reserved for the nobles and chiefs, but in general any animal which fell to the arrows of a rider was his trophy. Later Khans, to enliven the sport, would loose tigers in the circle and the riders would spur toward the snarling big cats, shooting arrow after arrow at their striped sides. Then as they passed the target, they turned in the saddle and shot backward, without any loss of efficiency, speed or accuracy. Even the sport of the horsemen was dangerous and calculated to suit them for war.

Later Chinese emperors, after the Mongols had been driven out and before the Manchus came riding in from the north, hunted in a much more sedate and less hazardous fashion. K'ang-hsi went out to hunt, after his days in the saddle, on an open palanquin. He sat cross-legged on an open platform, borne on the shoulders of four men, with his bow and a sheaf of arrows within easy reach. Wings of beaters walked out on either flank, to drive any game up in front of the emperor. The old man did not entirely trust his skill as an archer, for as insurance the platform also carried an old fowling piece, should the "Son of Heaven" miss with his arrows.

There were of course instances when the battle tactics such as those used by Kublai Khan against Nayan were not suited to the engagement. At such times the adaptability of the Mongols and the versatility of their commanders won or lost the struggle. Often the commanders were not Mongols but were drawn from among other nations. Their services and abilities were awarded with high position in the army. Such was the case with Nasr-ed-din, a Persian who served ably and well under Kublai Khan.

At one point Nasr-ed-din was in command of a body of twelve thousand veteran Mongol bowmen in a struggle to subdue what is now the province of Yunnan. His task was the subjugation of the various cities and tribes, and the imposition of imperial rule from Peking. Against his forces he found the army of the King of Mien and Bangala.

Scouts brought word to the Mongol camp that the enemy numbered sixty thousand troops, plus a formidable body of war elephants, each of which carried a howdah full of archers. From his camp in the hills, Nasr-ed-din surveyed the situation and decided to give battle on terrain which would best suit the traditional Mongol tactics. One factor disquieted the Persian mercenary's plans; the men of his command were totally trustworthy and quite prepared to go into battle in the face of such overwhelming odds, but the horses were another matter. How would the steppe ponies react to sight and smell of elephants?

Nasr-ed-din decided not to trust the horses too much under the circumstances and accordingly, when his men came down onto the flat lands along the banks of the Upper Irrawaddy, he drew up his lines so that one flank was protected by forest. The enemy, informed that the Mongols were out on the river plain, moved his troops forward, with the elephants in the van. At a considerable distance behind, he brought up his infantry and cavalry in two wings, which joined at the rear.

As the Mien forces advanced, sounding the usual array of trumpets and drums, the Mongols held firm in their position until the enemy was about 250 yards away. Then Nasr-ed-din gave the signal to charge, but the ponies were completely terrified by the elephants. The enemy continued to advance while the Mongol horse wheeled and turned, seeking to flee before the smell of the war elephants. Nasr-ed-din gave an order and instantly one man in ten took the horses of his group and went off into the forest. There the frightened animals were tethered, while the rest of the Mongols advanced on foot. Their aim was specifically for the elephants and, going right under the bellies of the great animals, they stung and goaded them with arrow fire. The archers in the howdahs tried to drive off the dismounted troopers, but their bows were lighter than the Mongols' and failed to penetrate their lacquered armor.

Even elephants are not arrow-proof, and on the tenth volley the beasts mutinied and fled from the field into the forest, knocking off their howdahs in their wild flight. As soon as the elephants deserted the field, the Mongols marched off into the trees and remounted their horses. Then they came back onto the river plain and proceeded to demolish the infantry and cavalry which had by then come into the line of battle.

Had the Mien forces been armored, the battle might have had a different outcome, but neither men nor elephants had any protection in the fight and this in combination with the greater power of the Mongol bows was sufficient to make it a complete victory for the forces of Kublai Khan. Nor must it be forgotten that Nasr-ed-din showed great acumen in his analysis of position and the adaptability which he displayed during the fighting.

Mongol tactics and strategy were, in their era, invincible. Arrow fire gave them superb missile power, horses gave them a mobility which was not successfully challenged. The lightning attack, coupled with planned total devastation, added the factor of psychology to their repertoire. When, on the eve of World War II, the German general staff wanted to plan an invincible arm, they studied the strategy and tactics of the Mongols before they arrived at the Panzer divisions which swept opposition before them as effortlessly as had their prototypes eight hundred years before. No greater nor more horrible tribute could have been paid to Temujin and his bow-bearing Sons of the Wolf.

While the empire of the Mongols extended into European Russia and as far south as India, we are apt to associate it most closely with China. We must also, in gathering a picture of Asiatic archery, turn to the other side of this continent, to Asia Minor and the Near East. Here the heirs of the Babylonians and of Alexander lived and fought. Here, too, the Crusaders came, intent on rescuing Jerusalem the Holy from the hands of Moslems.

The camel driver who became the Prophet of Allah preached a violent religion and it spread quickly along the Mediterranean littoral. Since war against the unbelievers was part of the Moslem scheme, their creed was spread with fire and sword and the bow. In fact it is even said that the Prophet himself was the possessor of three bows. But the bow was never the exclusive weapon of the proselytizing Moslems. Being opportunists, they availed themselves of every kind of weapon. If their converts were bowmen, they used the bow, but if their converts were swordsmen, the sword became their arm. Mohammedanism was warlike, but it was a religion.

The press of war and conquest in Central Asia, however, had the effect of driving numerous small tribes and hordes out of the center of the maelstrom, so that they spilled over into the lands which had, by then become largely Moslem. One such group were the Seljuk Turks, who so disastrously defeated the Byzantines. These wanderers came to a land and took service there as herdsmen or mercenaries. Then in time they established their own foothold in the country and almost imperceptibly became part of it.

Thus, during the time of the first Crusade, the iron-clad warriors from Europe found themselves up against the swift-moving riders who plied their bows to such effect. And at the Horns of Hattin, chivalry met its first great defeat. Never afterward could the forces of Christendom in the east muster such an army in the field as perished at Hattin.

It was in the year 1189 that the army of the Crusaders met the combined Moslem forces under the command of Saladin. The Kurdish chieftain, who was the spearhead of the attack against the Crusaders, had been attacking the castle of Tiberias with some twelve thousand men. Against them, the Kingdom of Jerusalem put into the field twelve hundred

knights, two thousand light cavalry and ten thousand infantry. The Crusaders, moving ill-advisedly, found themselves
in a position where it was necessary for them to dry-march
for about twenty miles across a desert known as the Djebel
Turan in order to reach the Sea of Galilee and water.

Saladin allowed the Crusaders to get deep into the desert
before he even moved. Then out of the dunes came troops of
light mounted bowmen, who pinned the Crusaders in position—and held them there. The heavily armed knights were
unable to come to grips with the Moslem forces, which
simply retreated whenever attack threatened. And there the
finest fighting force of the kingdom perished. On the second
day of the battle, Saladin brought up seventy full camel-loads
of arrows, so that his men would not fall short of ammunition. When the Crusaders, driven half mad by thirst, were
finally forced to move, their ranks were ragged, discipline
had evaporated in the sun and they perished before the rain
of Moselm arrows and finally under hewing Moslem swords.
There was no shortage of courage on the part of the Crusaders, but they had placed themselves in a totally untenable
position, where any movement, forward or back, exposed
them to the arrow fire and greater mobility of Saladin's men.
The shock power of the Crusaders had been proven time
and again—when they could actually meet the enemy. But
unless that meeting, with its terrific shock power, could be
effected, they were hopelessly outranged and defenseless before the swift moving, lightly armored bowmen.

Richard, the Lion Heart, who attempted to win back the
city of Jerusalem from Saladin, finally developed a counter-
move to these Moslem tactics. He realized that in this
type of warfare, it was almost as important to save the lives
of the horses as it was to preserve men. Once a knight was
unhorsed, the very weight of his equipment made him a
clumsy, slow-moving target, not even capable of keeping up
with his own brothers in arms. Therefore when Richard
marched south along the coast of Asia Minor after taking the

city of Acre, he tried to protect the horses as much as possible. To accomplish this he divided his forces into three columns: the weakest—women, children, wounded, baggage and supplies—moved closest to the shore; the knights—spearmen and swordsmen, on their heavy battle chargers were in the center; and on the inboard side, closest to the enemy marched the infantry, consisting mostly of bowmen and crossbowmen. As they marched they fired to their left, countering the whisking attacks of the Kurdish and Turkish cavalry, which stung at the marching men.

However, since the infantry was also armored, to a certain extent they were protected from the Moslem arrows. And their position in part relieved the pressure on the knights. If, however, the Moslems chose to charge in an attempt to cut down the infantry, the cavalry was in a position to come into contact with them. The combination of missile power, protected by potential shock power, saved the Crusaders' forces as they went south. It is significant that the English bows seem to have been heavier and with a consequent greater effective range in this protracted engagement, which served to keep the Moslem riders at bay.

Archery also played a large part in the one instance in which the Crusaders sided with the Moslems in battle. Dissension had split the Moslem ranks and Damascus found itself ranged against Egypt in a life-and-death struggle. The forces from the Nile had been considerably augmented by thousands of Khorasmians, fleeing from the Mongols. To counteract this combination, the Moslem lords of Damascus sent word to the Crusaders, asking for aid in driving out the Egyptians and their allies. The Crusaders responded by sending all their armed men and for once the knights of Christendom found common cause with their enemy.

The battle was fought at Gaza and remains one of the most decisive in the entire history of the Crusades. The command of the Egyptian forces fell on Baibars, the leader of the Mamelukes, and he deployed his forces to their maximum advantage. To meet the oncoming Moslem-Crusader army he placed his Khorasmian allies in his center and supported them on both flanks with bodies of Mamelukes.

The tactics which had been so advantageous on the steppes were equally effective here and after the arrows had done their work, the Khorasmians charged through the center of the Crusaders' line, then wheeled back and broke the supporting Moslem flank. Gaza was an overwhelming victory for the Egyptians and amply illustrated the fact that in open combat not even full armor was sufficient defense against practically ceaseless arrow fire, followed by shock.

Although the Crusaders numbered many bowmen and crossbowmen in their ranks, at no time did they essay to put into the field a force which relied on these weapons primarily. And although they suffered sorely on this account, the Christian leaders seemingly would not or could not learn to change their mode of fighting. There are several factors involved in this lack of adaptability. First and foremost, the Crusaders did not produce any significant military leaders— examination of the records shows that while there were many good soldiers and thousands of courageous fighters, there was no single military genius, capable of evaluating terrain, climate and psychology so as to convert his own forces into an arm capable of meeting the Moslem bowmen on their own level. Secondly even under what was mediocre command, the thinking of the leaders was along the lines of chivalry, which meant shock and precluded reliance on missiles to any appreciable extent. There was a tendency on the part of the knights to feel that their mission of salvation was based on single combat, with all the trappings, and that the efforts of the common soldier with his bow or ax were a necessary evil. Missile warfare was for the peasantry, and in those years the peasantry counted for but little.

And by the time the Crusaders had lived long enough in what came to be called Outremer, to adopt indigenous arms and tactics, they had lost the tremendous drive which had sparked the efforts of their fathers and grandfathers. Every time new and decisive moves were made by the Christian force, it came as a direct result of new blood, new men, new arms flowing in from Europe. And so, as far as the bow was concerned, it was always a secondary weapon in the minds of the Crusaders.

Not so with the Moslems, who through constant contact with the Mongols and Tartars, through tribal migrations and through cultural exchanges at every level, became more and more proficient at archery. Mongols under Genghis Khan took and held Persia, and when the Pope failed to make any sustained efforts to convert the Mongols to Christianity, the Moslems leaped into the gap and converted the Mongol shahs. When the Turks came out of Central Asia, they too fell under Moslem domination and since the two nations controlled almost the entirety of the Middle East, they became as a matter of course both archery-conscious and Moslem. More correctly, they were already archers and became Mohammedans. Even Egypt, which is geographically African, became Turkish in thought and culture, so that in an analysis of archery in Asia, we must allow consideration for Egyptian bowmen.

Tamerlane, or Timur Leng, was the second of the great Mongol conquerors, but since this is a history of archery and not of peoples or wars, we need only say that the Timurid empire followed closely on the pattern established by Attila and Genghis Khan. Actually it more closely resembled the former, for at the death of The Lame One, his empire passed into oblivion. Only in India was there any lasting Mongol influence, in the form of the Mogul rulers, who were ultimately defeated by the English, and these were descendants of Timur Leng, rather than immediate heirs.

Tamerlane mustered the tribes once more, in response to the lure of loot and empire. Under his banner rode Turcomans and Turkis, Kazaks and Uigurs, Buriats and Kankalis and a hundred other tribes. Once more the mounted bowmen swept across two continents, making a desolation of cities and a memory of nations. Where Genghis Khan had attempted to establish a regime which would last, Tamerlane allowed a sense of personal aggrandizement to lead him, and while his empire rose phoenixlike from the ashes of his conquests, it was a fleeting thing, lacking the administrative and organizational brilliance which had marked the rule of Genghis Khan and his immediate successors.

Archery continued to play an active part in Mid-Asiatic life long after Tamerlane and his dreams of glory. Although the conversion of the Mongol tribes to Lamaite Buddhism marked the end of their most warlike activities, they continued to be a pastoral people. And clinging as they did to their old ways, they continued to use the bow extensively. As late as the 1930's the bow played an active part in the lives of the men of the steppes.

The Mongolian influences in Europe are almost exclusively confined to Russia, since any Hunnish remains in Hungary have long been assimilated in the bulk of the total population. Russia, on the other hand, was for so long under Mongol influence in varying degrees that it is still readily apparent to the anthropologist and the psychologist.

As Russia in Europe began to grow under the power of the Tsars, she expanded to the east, and this, in combination with the remnants of the early Hordes, made her extremely conscious of Mongolian archery. At one point during this eastward expansion, a Russian force of invaders and colonists encountered the Usbec Tartars, who had ridden under both Genghis Khan and Tamerlane. The Europeans were well equipped with the best muskets of the time and well supplied with powder and ball, but in a series of running fights, the troops with their wagonloads of settlers were compelled to retreat entirely from the Usbec territory. The muskets were outranged by the Usbec bows, which were effective for at least a hundred paces farther. The Tsars did not forget the efficacy of the Usbecs and enlisted as many Mongols as possible in the imperial army. During Napoleon's retreat from Moscow, Bashkir Tartars were the most valuable troops in the entire Russian army. Ranging through the deep winter snows with complete ease and living entirely off the country, their heavy bows and deadly shafts played havoc with the Napoleonic troops as they beat their way homeward. At another period in Bashkir history, a body of mounted archers from another territory invaded one of their camps and captured all the people there. No men were at the camp during the raid and the coup appeared to be a complete success until the raiders were set upon by one lone Bashkir archer. Outranging the invaders by a good distance, he soon was able to cut their forces to ribbons and succeeded in freeing all his people.

Another people who enjoyed a considerable reputation as archers during Tsarist times were the Samoyeds, from the Siberian tundra. During the late seventeenth century, the Tsar had two Samoyeds brought from their homes to Moscow to give an exhibition of their skill with the bow. Before the Imperial Russian Court, these two swarthy nomads from the land of snow and ice repeatedly hit coins with hunting arrows from a distance which was so great that observers could barely distinguish the targets.

No doubt today the Communist regime in both Russia and China has blotted out the last remains of the old ways, but in 1938 Mongol hunters went armed with the bow in eastern Manchuria, and the tribes of Harar marked a marriage by placing a bow and a full quiver atop the bridal tent. However, after the two great Mongol conquerors, the people themselves lapsed into obscurity and we must travel back to Persia and Turkey to find the full flowering of Asiatic archery.

Both the Turks and the Persians inherited their love of archery from their ancestors. As we have seen in a previous chapter, the original Persians, who came from the steppes, were bowmen, and so it was with the Turks, coming in from the same areas. Both the Seljuk and Osmanli, who became known as the Ottomans, were archers by instinct and heredity. Both nations used the bow from necessity and in later centuries brought to it a devotion which almost amounted to fanaticism.

When the Turks had finally become settled in their new homes and when the pressures of the Mongols had receded from Persia, the men of these two nations devoted themselves to archery to an extent never matched before or since. What baseball is to the United States and cricket is to England, archery was to Turkey and Persia. Whole sections of cities supported themselves by bowyery and fletching and in Persia one bowyer became immortal. He was Chaeh, granted the gift of eternal life because his bows were always waterproof. Since all these bows were composites—some of them had as many as five elements, their water-repelling qualities were vital.

War and training for war furnished the main occupations of the majority. Unlike England, where the bow was the weapon of the common man, in the Orient the bow was considered the queen of weapons—sultans, shahs, khans and ilkhans prided themselves on their prowess. In fact, what is still the longest arrow flight on record was made by the Sultan of Turkey. The shot, made at the end of the eighteenth century, was witnessed by the then English Ambassador to the Sublime Porte, Sir Robert Ainslie. Using a bow pulling well over one hundred pounds and using flight arrows, the sultan succeeded in driving one shaft for a distance of 972 yards. In European and American minds there seems always to have been some question as to the authenticity of this shot, yet somehow it seems rather strange to question the word of an ambassador, who stood to gain little or nothing by attesting to a false record. Perhaps the question rises in our minds because of the simple fact that we have fallen woefully short in trying to equal or better the distance ever since. The closest is the flight record established in

1955 by Charles Pierson. Using a "free-style" bow, Pierson shot 768 yards. "Free-style" in this case meant that the archer put his feet in stirrups on either side of the bow handle and used both hands to draw the string. It is a recognized method of shooting in the United States, although our English cousins look down their noses at us for the practice, claiming that the act simply turns the shooter into a "human crossbow." Although the Turks were familiar with this style of shooting, there is nothing in the record to indicate that the sultan used a foot bow, but simply that he possessed the ability to use a bow with what we would classify as an almost unusable draw weight. Everything we know about archery in Turkey and Persia points to the fact that all archers were trained with bows of an enormous pull. Some of the records are so fantastic as to make us seriously doubt their validity. For example, in the seventeenth century, the Chevalier Cliardin visited the court of the Shah of Persia and watched the training of young bowmen there: "some of their bows are exceedingly strong; and the method they make use of to know their power, is by fastening them to a support driven into the wall, and suspending weights to the string at the point where the arrow is placed . . ." This in itself is nothing but a variation of the method we ourselves use in determining the draw of a bow, but when the chevalier goes on, ". . . The strongest require five hundred pounds weight, to draw them up to the arrow's point," we begin to wonder. Howard Hill pulls a bow of over one hundred pounds, but it is extremely doubtful if there are three men in the world today who could draw—and use—a bow pulling over two hundred pounds. We cannot, however, discount Cliardin's account entirely, since he does go on to give us a clue as to how this remarkable performance was achieved, ". . . when the pupils can manage the common bow, they then have another given them, which they make heavier and heavier by means of large iron rings which are placed on the string. . . ." It would be interesting to try an experiment, just to see if a young archer using such a system would finally be able to draw and use a five-hundred-pound bow.

Our custom of marking the draw weight of the bow on one of the limbs seems to have been imported from China. About two hundred years ago, all Chinese bows were of four draw weights: seventy pounds, eighty pounds, ninety pounds and one hundred. Anything over that weight was for show or for special types of shooting: Each class of bow was marked according to its weight and the custom spread to the Occident from there.

While the Turks did not customarily use foot bows for flight shooting, they did, however, have one "aid" which is not used in America or Europe. It was a horn or ivory 'bow trough,' fastened to the back of the bow hand, which had the effect of lengthening the arrows. In order to understand its function fully, we must remember that the Turks, like most Orientals, shot with the shaft to the right of the bow. This is directly the reverse of our practice, where the arrow rests on the left, or outside of the bow. The horn groove was attached to the back of the bow hand by leather straps and met the bow exactly where the arrow crossed. Thus, when the arrow was drawn it continued past the inside of the bow and was held in position by the trough. On the release, the arrow shot out in a normal fashion, having gained as much additional cast as the "overdraw" would give. Such a method permits the use of arrows which are very short, proportionally, to the bow used. Thus a twenty-four-inch arrow could be cast as effectively as a normal twenty-eight-inch shaft. In 1792 one of the under secretaries of the Turkish Embassy in London set a flight record using such a trough. The record was to stand for almost 150 years, discounting the sultan's mark. Mahmoud Effendi shot in Hyde Park on a hot July afternoon and against the wind made a mark of 415 yards. With the wind he was able to better the flight to the extent of 482 yards. The bow had a draw of 160 pounds and the arrow measured twenty-five and one-half inches. By means of the groove, Mahmoud Effendi pulled three inches inside the bow, thereby in effect shooting an arrow of twenty-eight and one-half inches. After the display, Mahmoud Effendi apologized for not setting a better mark, saying that at home he had bettered the distance often and that he was not by any means the best flight shot in Turkey.

Such excellence cannot be achieved without constant practice, beginning early in life. As their nomad ancestors had done, the Persians and Turks taught their sons to ride and shoot from infancy. Cliardin's account speaks of some of the feats which were part of the Persian archery curriculum, "The pupils draw, string and unstring their bows while they leap and jump about, sometimes while they stand on one leg, sometimes on their knees and sometimes while running at full speed. . . . The modern exercise of the bow, as a pastime, is performed by them on horseback as well as on foot. The horseman gallops away with the bow and arrow in his hand, and when he has reached a certain point, he inclines either to the right or left, and discharges his arrows, which to win a prize must hit a cup fixed at the top of a pole about 120 feet in height." Such practices were almost universal in the Middle East and we see the Mamelukes in Cairo giving a similar performance. Here, mounted bowmen passed at full gallop between two targets, discharging their arrows from side to side, and scoring with every shot. Other archers, to prove their dexterity, unstrung their bows, whirled them about their heads by the bowstrings, restrung the bows and then shot with deadly accuracy—all while their horses were moving at top speed. The finale of the display came with one rider standing straddle on two running horses. He shot three arrows at the target as he approached and three more as he raced away. All six arrows were direct hits.

This practice of shooting behind was a favorite with all the horse archers of Asia. It is entirely probable that the Huns used it in battle, and the Parthians were famous for it. In fact, it has passed into the language in the form of the phrase "a Parthian shot." The men of Genghis Khan and Tamerlane were well versed in such shooting and here again we find horse archers practicing to perfect the tactic. The European traveler Busbequius described the training for the "Parthian shot."

"They erect a high pole in the center of a plain, having a small brass ball fixed on its top. Around this pole they spur vigorously until they are a little beyond it, with the horse still galloping. Suddenly they turn in their splendid morocco saddles and drive an arrow into the globe, even as they fly. The constant practice of this maneuver renders them so expert that, the bow being turned in the sight of the unwary pursuer, he is instantly shot through and through by their arrows."

Another favorite training method was for the rider to attach a length of rope to his saddle. Fixed to the end of this rope was a small object, shaped rather like a dumbbell. As the horse galloped along, the movement of the dumbbell gave the archer ample scope to test his accuracy. Archers were taught to shoot from every conceivable position and also to string the bows under adverse conditions. Since the bows were, as we have said, of a very heavy draw weight, these exercises were often difficult. One treatise in Arabic lists over forty positions which can be used in stringing the bow, ranging from one where the archer is sitting up to his waist in water, to one where the bow is held directly over the head. In connection with the heaviest bows, the Turkish archers used a device called the *kemend*. This was a long leather strap which went around the archer's waist from back to front. The two ends of the strap or thong were then fixed to the nocks or "ears" of the bow, and the archer braced his feet against the belly of the bow, at the same time pulling back with his body. As the bow came into position the string was slipped up with the fingers into the nocks and the *kemend* afterward disengaged.

Turkish and Persian arrows were masterpieces of the fletcher's craft. The flight arrows, with which they set so many records, were all slightly barreled, that is, their maximum dimension was in midshaft with a slight taper from there toward either end. Hunting and war shafts were of a more ordinary design, like our own, with the dimension of the shaft remaining constant. The Persians used several types of arrow, some made of wood and some of reed or bamboo. In Arabic the reed arrows were known as *schem* and the wood shafts were called *neschab*. The word for bow, or more properly the bow, is *El Kus*. The Persians also made a fine distinction between arrows that were used for war and hunting and which were recoverable and the lighter practice shafts which were properly "losers." The Turks, on the other hand, made most of their shafts from red fir. Both nations used a variety of heads, suited to the type of shooting involved. Most of the target arrows were headed with a pyramidal form, easily extracted from the wet mud walls which served in many cases as targets.

In Persia the mark was often fixed to a high pole and was, for practice, a ripe melon which would split when hit. In competitive shooting the melon was replaced with a bag of leather filled with silver or gold coins, which were the reward of the successful marksmen.

During a rebellion in the hill provinces of Persia, the leader of the revolt was captured and the shah determined to make an example of his captive. Accordingly the man was first shod with molten iron and then hoisted to the top of the archers' mast. Then the shah galloped past and planted an arrow in the victim's body. At this signal the rest of the court rode across the arena, firing as they went, so that within minutes the captive's body resembled a pincushion swinging from the top of the pole.

Constant practice with the bow made for a great number of expert marksmen and even the rulers were credited with a high degree of skill. To impress European visitors to his

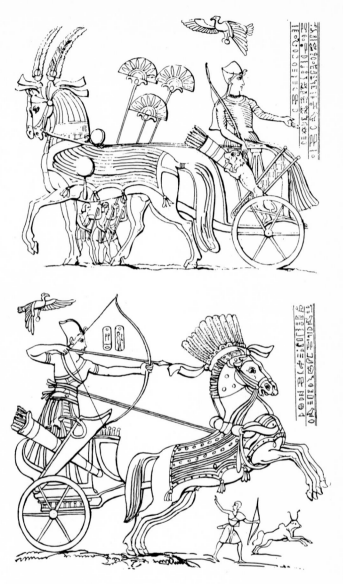

Egyptian. Although many of the illustrations in George A. Hansard's books were inaccurate, this is very accurate.

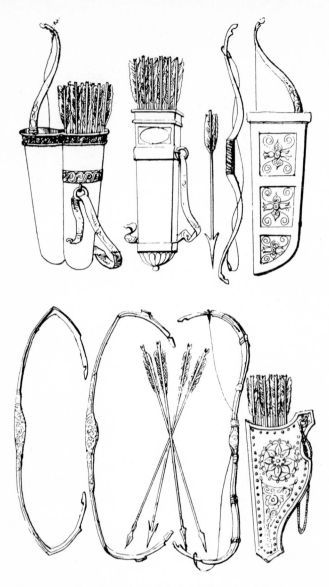

Grecian and Oriental Tackle. Grecian (top) is not too accurate, but the Oriental is a very good reproduction of mid-Asiatic bows and quivers. The combination bow case and quiver was originated by the Scythians and was called a "gortyus."

Top: The "Parthian Shot," described in text.

Bottom: African. These pictures are typical of the artistry of the era (1840). Obviously the right-hand is "The Noble Savage."

Assyrian. Although listed as Egyptian, the picture is almost pure Assyrian.

Roman archers. The armor and bows are completely anachronistic. If considered from post-Republican Rome, bows are accurate but the dress of the archers is unrealistic.

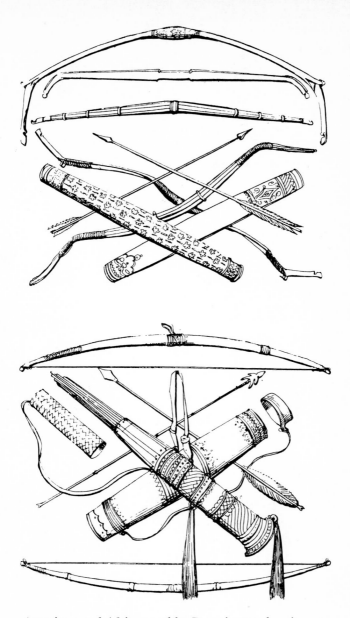

American and African tackle. Bows in top drawing are African, probably of Egyptian origin for they show the Asiatic influence. Bottom picture is a fairly good representation of South American equipment.

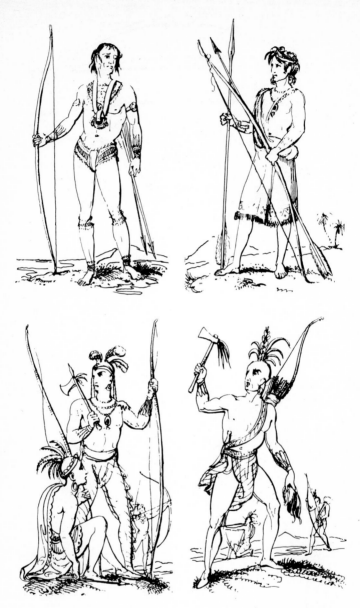

South and North American Indians. These are pretty pictures, but inaccurate. No tribe dressed the way the Indian is depicted in the lower right-hand picture or carried that type of bow. The extreme length of the arrows in the upper right picture is correct for many South American tribes, but the costume is inaccurate.

Saxon and Norman archers. These drawings are accurate both as to costume and equipment. The top two pictures are Saxon and the lower is Norman. The Norman bow is a little too long for complete accuracy, and it is also doubtful that the Normans drew to the face.

Chinese and Tartar archers. These pictures are very
accurate, but are primarily Chinese rather than Tartar.

court, one native ruler ordered a slave to hold a ring suspended by horsehair at a distance of twenty paces. Then he deliberately drew his bow and cut the horsehair, six times in succession. On another occasion, Europeans in Constantinople watched mounted archers in a demonstration of their prowess. After the usual display of trick shooting, one of the riders ordered a slave forward into the center of the riding grounds. On the head of the slave he placed an orange and, racing past, split the fruit with his arrow. So pleased was the archer with his success that he repeated the stunt twice more, never harming the slave in the least. It was at this same exhibition that the riders aimed and hit consistently the hind shoes of the horse galloping immediately in front.

This preoccupation with all forms of archery led to an almost religious devotion to the art, either as a pastime or as a facet of war. In early days a strung bow passing among the clans served as the signal for war. Later the beautiful bows, with their gold and silver chasings, often carried short quotations from the Koran, the holy book of the Moslems. Bows were highly valued and in addition to the homilies engraved on them, they also bore the owner's name in the same flowing Arabic script. We can get some idea of the value placed on bows when we find that they were considered a royal gift. The Shah of Persia at one time sent a gift of nine bows, and arrows for each, to the Ottoman sultan, Amurath. And the Dutch East Indian Company, seeking to curry favor with the kingdom of Ceylon in 1656, bought in Persia six bows and sets of arrows to present to the Ceylonese king.

Royal arrows were often fletched with the wing feathers of eagles, although at one time such fletching was sought throughout the Oriental world. The city of Babadagy, according to Marco Polo, "derived no trifling advantage from trading in eagles' wings, as that bird frequents a neighboring mountain in vast numbers. The arrow makers throughout Persia and Tartary are all supplied from thence. They (these feathers) are esteemed superior to all others for winging arrows and a skillful archer does not care to use any other. If a man has several shafts in his quiver, with other feathers, and but one among them fletched with an eagle's quill, that one, remaining untouched, will eat all the rest to the wood." As eagles were hunted for their feathers, they grew scarcer in consequence, and finally the presentation of a set of eagle-fletched arrows came to be a truly regal present. Strangely enough, the superstition which Marco Polo relates about the corrosive quality of eagle feathers remained current for centuries. As late as the nineteenth century it was believed that some unknown substance in an eagle feather would eat away any other feather brought into contact with it.

Oriental bowstrings were almost always made of silk. Strands were laid for the string's length until the resulting mass was about the thickness of "a goose quill." Then the string was whipped, in a contrasting color, for about three inches at the nocking point and at both ends. Sometimes tiny pennants of silk were woven into the whipping at the nocking point, but this was reserved for show and was seldom found in the hunting and war bows. Oriental bowstrings strike an oddly sinister note in history, since they were a favored instrument of execution in court intrigue. The string was held between the two hands, which were crossed, and the loop of the string was passed around the victim's neck. Used thus, the honest bowstring became the weapon of the strangler.

Expert pistol shots of today might be interested in the fact that the extreme, hand-fitting grip used on their weapons was adapted from a Turkish archery idea. The flight shooters were in the habit of taking long folds of muslin, impregnating them with warm wax and wrapping the whole mass around the bow handle. When the archer gripped the material, still in its plastic state, it took the form of his hand contour, thus giving him a grip which was entirely personal. After the wax had set, the grip or *muschamma* was removed and set aside for the archer, so that at all times his was a custom grip.

Asia provides us with a picture of archery at its historical peak. Nowhere else in the world has the bow played quite such an important part in the shaping of events. Even after the bow ceased to be a consequential weapon in the middle of the fifteenth century, it remained the treasured arm of the hunter and the athlete.

We have steadily advanced toward the mark set for us by the sultan in his often-doubted shot, and perhaps we may even equal what the Turks hold to be their record. But we still have a long way to go before we equal the penetration of one Persian shaft which is reported to have penetrated two inches of brass. Modern archery owes much to the basic design of the bow used in Asia and history would be far less colorful without the hordes of horse archers who have ridden across our pages.

7

The Yeomen Bowmen

WHENEVER ENGLISH ARCHERY IS MENTIONED, TWO FIGURES spring to mind—the bowmen who at Crécy, Poitiers and Agincourt defeated the might of European chivalry, and Robin Hood, the legendary archer bandit.

Behind the successes of the first, the English yeoman with his deadly longbow, lies an interesting chapter in the history of the bow. Archery was not apparently indigenous to the British Isles, and the date of its introduction into England is highly problematical. One common story says that archery was unknown to the English until the time of the Danish reaver kings Horsa and Hengist, who brought it to the island. Actually while this sounds good, it is probably far from true, since archery must certainly have been known in England, if not widely practiced, long before the raids of the Danes.

Two years before his assault on England, Julius Caesar in his wars against the Belgae, lists Cretan and Numidian archers among the auxiliary troops under his command—a fact we have already noted. Since the use of these archer mercenaries continued throughout the history of Roman Britain, it is only logical to suspect that the early English were well acquainted with the bow and its uses, if they themselves were not active participants.

One gets the feeling that archery was never really popular in England, either under Roman occupation or during the period which followed. There are scattered references to the use of the bow, but in the main it seems to have been reserved as an instrument of sport, somewhat beneath the dignity of the Saxon warrior, who was content to go into battle with sword, shield and battle ax.

Such an attitude is typical of all European military history, for if a god of battle were chosen to represent Europe's armed might it would certainly be Achilles, the Spearman, rather than the archer god Apollo. From a psychological standpoint, one concludes that the majority of Continental warfare was dependent on the hand-held weapon, rather than the missile, at least until the intrusion of gunpowder. The amazing defeats inflicted by bowmen were the exceptions which seemed to prove the rule. During those long centuries the control and waging of war was in the hands of the aristocracy, who considered it beneath them to think of fighting with missile weapons. It remained for the commoner to seize upon and use, to its best advantage, the weapon of archery.

Shortly after the Roman evacuation of Britian, and before the major Danish raids, we begin to find scattered references to the use of the bow. In the year 633 A.D., Offrid, son of Edwin, king of Northumbria, went into battle with his father's men against a combined army of Welsh and Mercians. The battle in nowise affected the over-all course of English history but it is recorded that Offrid died of an arrow wound, and because of later events it is fairly safe to assume that the archer or archers in the case were Welsh.

A little over two hundred years later, the Danes had not only raided deeply into the island, but here and there had established semipermanent holdings. In 870 the Danes fought against the Anglian king, Edmund, and defeated the Angles decisively. Part of their booty was the person of the king himself, and he was tied to a tree and used for a target by both Danish archers and javelin men. If one were to exchange the horned helmets and body armor of the Danes for the feathers and war paint of the American Indian, the scene would not have been unlike those repeated hundreds of times during the settlement of the United States, where prisoners served as a mark for the warriors and young men of the tribe. Neither barbarism nor archery was the exclusive property of any one nation or race.

In the early years of this century an unusually violent storm struck England. The tree which by tradition had served as Edmund's stake was severely wrenched and twisted by the accompanying high winds. The process served to work loose ancient and rusting arrowheads from deep in the trunk, and historians who had doubted the story of Danish targetry were forced to revise their opinions.

Under the legendary King Alfred, archery seems to have been more extensively used by the Saxons. In the famous scene where the warrior king allowed the scones to burn, he was daydreaming while he put his archery tackle into shape for the coming battle. And the chronicler Polydore Vergil, in describing the battle array of the period, speaks of a great number of archers used in the right wing of the army under Ethelred, the brother of Alfred. Unfortunately Vergil neglects to tell us whether these archers were Saxons, Angles or even Welsh.

The Welsh adopted archery earlier and with more zeal than any of the other tribes on the island. We have already seen, in the story of the death of Offrid, a case where the Welsh were supposedly using the bow as early as the seventh century. Again, shortly before the Battle of Hastings, there is a record of the Welsh use of the bow, contained in the *Anglo-Saxon Chronicle*. Ralph, Earl of Hereford, led a body of mounted Saxons in to the mountains of Wales to put down a revolt there. Deep in the hills the mounted men were received with such a volley of arrows that "before any spear had been thrown the English army fled, because they were on horseback." Hereford's men learned early the lessons of Crécy, three hundred years later—mounted men, unsupported by long-range missiles, could not face well-equipped and disciplined archers. In fact, they could not even make contact.

Again, in the same *Anglo-Saxon Chronicle* there is a specific statement about the current attitude on archery. It says that among the English "archery although practiced as a sport is but little used in war." The bow then was accounted good for the felling of red deer, boar, bear and wolves but held a little use against an armed man.

Although it was far too late, the English might have learned the advantage of archery from a battle fought immediately prior to Hastings. Vikings were raiding in the north of the country, and the English, under Harold, finally brought them to bay at what is now the town of Stamford Bridge. The Viking king, Harald Hardrada, held off the forces of Harold of England by retreating within a shield wall or shield burgh and driving off his attackers with arrows. Time after time attacks withered before the arrow fire and when the English ultimately broke through the shield burgh and killed the invaders, it was due more to a failure of ammunition than to any other single cause. The Vikings ran short of arrows, and their attempts to sally out of the shield fort were useless.

At Hastings the Anglo-Saxons were again confronted with archers, although in this instance they were used offensively rather than defensively. Throughout the battle, Harold's men adopted a defensive position and, had they not broken from it, the entire history of England might have been changed. The Norman use of archery was extensive but it does not seem to have been a very decisive factor in the over-all pattern of the battle.

Here it was the Normans who came up against the shield burgh and time after time failed to pierce it. Late in the afternoon William of Normandy ordered his archers to raise their arrows so that the shafts would fall among the heads of the Anglo-Saxons. To defend themselves, they raised their shields, thereby breaking the line of the wall. The immediate result of this maneuver was the death of Harold of England, who died with an arrow in his eye, shot in high arc by some Norman bowman.

The Norman victory was greatly assisted by the death of Harold, but if the English had not followed a feigned retreat of the Normans, the hill of Seulac would have been defendable. The death of an individual commander from an arrow does not mean that archery was a great factor in the battle.

One of the truly amazing things about the Battle of Hastings lies in the variety of accounts. Although it has been proved that archery was well known to the English, some of the writers speak of the effect of arrows coming as a surprise to the Anglo-Saxons. Echard says, "The fight began with great fury, order and equal bravery on both sides; in which the English were severely galled by the thick showers of arrows from the Norman longbows, before the battle was joined; which was a weapon unused in England, thereby the more surprising: the wounds coming from enemies so far distant, and not suddenly to be revenged." While the English may not have used the bow as a war weapon, this account appears to be utterly ludicrous, for they had certainly seen the effects of arrows shot from a distance, long before Norman William beat them on the hill of Seulac. These were the same troops which a week or two before had stood with Harold at Stamford Bridge under the steady fire of Viking shafts.

Strictly speaking, the use of the word "longbow" in connection with the Normans is incorrect. The Normans used a comparatively short bow. The longbow as we know it is an English development, coming after the Conquest. The chroniclers of the time used the term "longbow" to distinguish it from the crossbow.

The Conquest was, however, the deciding factor in the growth of English archery. Heretofore, the bow had been the arm of the hunter, the weapon of the invader and the wild Welsh, but now it assumed a new importance. Under William and his successors, the Saxons felt the yoke of invasion and occupation and they were expressly forbidden the use of "knightly" weapons. Seeking the arms for rebellion, they turned more and more to the hitherto despised bow and arrows, particularly since they were inexpensive and easily made from materials at hand. Horses and armor might be forbidden but the stuff of bows and "clothe-yard shafts" grew all about and, used expertly, were perhaps even deadlier. Under Norman rule, the Saxons made common ground with the rebellious Welsh and found in them expert tutors in the fine art of archery.

William Rufus, called Red Beard, son of the Conquerer, was slain by an arrow while hunting deer in the New Forest. Accounts of the shooting differ, some holding the weapon to have been a longbow while others say that it was a crossbow. Even the name of the regicide changes—Sir Walter Tyrell in some, and plain Watt Tyrell in others. It is probable, however, that he was slain by a crossbow quarrel and accidentally. But the longbow, or its immediate progenitor, was already well established as an English weapon by the time of the civil wars under King Stephen and Queen Maude, where we find numerous mentions of the use of archers, not crossbowmen, in battle.

Stephen often fought against the Scots, and at Cuton Moor in Yorkshire, he won his fight by the use of arrows. Moving into position, Stephen was driven back by the claymore-swinging Scots, but on his retreat his lightly clad bowmen began to put volley after volley of arrows into the Scottish ranks, finally routing them completely and driving them from the field. As one chronicle recounts, "the English terribly galled the Galwegians (a then current name for the Lowland Scots) and obliged them to quit their posts, after they had compelled his men-at-arms to give way."

Within a hundred years of the Conquest the breach between Saxon and Norman was somewhat healed, and we find English infantry of the time consisting largely of archers, with some slingers. The conquest of Ireland, in 1172, would not have been possible without the use of the longbow. Henry II granted permission to certain lords to seize the island and under the leadership of Richard, Earl of Clare and Pembroke, better known as Strongbow, the conquest was begun. As Lord Lyttelton says, the bow seems to have been introduced into Ireland during this campaign, and he remarks, "It is strange that the Irish, who had much intercourse with the Welsh (they were in fact cousins) before the time of Henry II, should not have learnt from that nation, who greatly excelled in archery, that arrows were better weapons to annoy the enemy with than stones, which unless at a small distance, could have little or no effect . . . from many instances in the course of these wars, it appears that the English conquests in Ireland were principally owing to the use of the longbow in battle, which the Irish infantry wanted."

Strongbow, in spite of his titles and rights, preferred, during battle, to dismount and fight among his archers. He himself drew the heaviest bow in England, with abnormally long arms. And so Ireland fell to the bow in the hands of the invader, as England had fallen a hundred years before.

During this same period, the reign of Henry II, we get a vivid picture of medieval archery. The writer Giraldus Cambrensis, going into Wales during the preachment of a Crusade, noted somewhat of the practice in that country. "There is a particular tribe in Wales named the Venta; a people brave and warlike, and who far excel the other inhabitants of that country in the practice of archery. During a siege, it came about that two soldiers, running in haste towards a tower, situated some little distance from them, were attacked with a number of arrows from the Welsh; which being shot with prodigious violence, some penetrated through the oak doors of a portal, although they were the breadth of four fingers in thickness. The heads of these arrows were afterwards driven out and preserved, in order to continue the rememberance of such extraordinary force in shooting with the bow. . . . It happened also in a battle, in the time of William de Breuas, as he himself relates, that a Welshman, having directed his arrow at a horse soldier who was clad in armour and had his leathern coat under it, the arrow, beside piercing the man through the hip, struck also in the saddle and mortally wounded the horse on which he sat. Another Welsh soldier, having shot an arrow at a horseman who was covered with strong armour in the same manner the shaft penetrated through his hip and fixed it in the saddle, what is most remarkable is, that as the horseman drew his bridle aside to turn around, he received another arrow in his hip on the opposite side, which, passing through it, he was firmly fastened to the saddle on both sides."

The "knightly" weapons, denied the English but a short while before, were obviously no match for the power and penetration of the longbow and the "clothe-yard shaft." The succeeding kings, recognizing the value of such weapons, did everything in their power to foster the use of the bow. The extent of this royal indulgence is evidenced by a statute of the period which literally forgave a man murder—if the victim passed between an archer and his practice targets.

The now fully developed longbow was without peer as a missile weapon in the Occidental world and continued so, long after the development and primary use of gunpowder. In fact, it was not until the development of an efficient repeating rifle in the middle of the last century that the bow was really superseded as a rapid-fire, accurate weapon. Where the crossbow, in its military version, may have had a superior range (and even this is open to question), its rate of fire was so comparatively slow that it was in actuality a far inferior weapon. By the same token the hunting crossbow was not as efficient as a hunting weapon not only by reason of its slowness, but often on account of its noise as well.

The skill and deadliness of the English archer was not a

matter of chance. Behind it lay years and years of practice, often beginning in infancy. Sir Arthur Conan Doyle, in *The White Company* gives us a picture of the training in those times when he describes two boys standing in front of their home, holding unshaped billets of bow wood, for hours at a time. The law prescribed the bow weights which were proper for youths of various ages. It is small wonder, then, that the yeomen of England could pull a war bow of one hundred pounds or more with ease and skill. Unfortunately very few bows from this period are still in existence, although in 1955 part of a longbow was found in the moat of an English castle. Modern archers who have examined the relic feel sure that when whole, the bow must have pulled nearly two hundred pounds with a twenty-eight- or thirty-inch shaft. The length of the arrows has been the subject of controversy for many years but today most authorities agree that they corresponded to the twenty-eight-inch shaft of the present, although in some instances they may have been longer. The former school, which believed the shafts to have been thirty-seven inches long, is now fallen somewhat into disrepute. The fletching of these arrows was largely goose, with gray the favored color.

The bows themselves were of many woods. The best was, of course, yew, but since little yew suitable for bows grew in England, most staves were imported, at prices which often put them beyond the means of the average man. So other native woods were often substituted, including elm. Pulling on an average one hundred pounds, the war bow was six feet long and usually self-nocked. That is, the nocks for the string, top and bottom, were integral parts of the bow itself. Fancier bows had horn or ivory nocks, fastened to the ends of the bow limbs. In cross section the longbow looked like a letter D lying on its back. The belly of the bow, facing the shooter, formed the round of the D, and the back, facing the target, was flat. Although from a standpoint of design the longbow was wasteful of both wood and energy, the English used it without knowing that fact, and it seems not to have detracted from its usefulness in the least. Bowstrings of the era were made of a good grade of flax or linen and, when strung, were impregnated with beeswax, so as to repel rain and dew.

The average bowman carried a sheaf of twenty-four arrows, in a belt quiver. The shoulder quiver seems to have been primarily a development of the American Indian. In battle the shafts were taken out of the quiver and placed, head first, in the ground immediately before the archer, within easy reach of his free hand.

During the period when Richard I was king of England we have few accounts of English archery. Gibbon, in his *Decline and Fall of the Roman Empire* mentions one instance, however, when Richard's archers proved their worth far from home. The figures seem wildly improbable, yet Gibbon is usually considered a reputable source. He says that Richard was defeated by Saladin at Jaffa and retreated to sea with his men. Under forced sail the English forces moved up the coast of the Holy Land to Acre and landed. The arrival of the English ships surprised the defenders and apparently scared off a body of sixty thousand Moslem soldiers, mostly light cavalry.

Richard, with what seems to have been his usual temerity, remained outside the walls of Acre during the night with a body of three hundred archers and seventeen knights. The following morning the Moslem host returned and were again driven off by the English. Odds of two hundred to one seem terrifically disproportionate, particularly since many of the Moslem soldiers in the Crusades were themselves horse archers of no mean ability. But while we may quarrel with the authenticity of Gibbon's figures in this case, we cannot dispute the fact that the English archers did repel the Moslems at Acre in this instance, in spite of terrific odds. In another section we have already seen how Richard made good use of his bowmen in the Crusades, so while the records are few, it is readily apparent that archery was still vitally important.

At home in England, Richard's reign is supposed to have coincided with the appearance of that most legendary archer of all time—Robin Hood. To many the name is synonymous with archery, and although fact may never be totally distinguished from fiction, Robin Hood will always remain dear, both to the archer and to the story teller.

The historians Holinshed and Stow both mention the feats of Robin Hood and the name occurs in another book of the period, the *Scotichronicon*. However, the most complete account is to be found in the works of a Scottish historian named John Maior, or Johannes Major. Maior was copied by Grafton, who in his *Chronicle of Breteyne*, says:

"About this time (1189) as sayth John Maior, in his chronicle of Scotland, there were many robbers and outlawes in England, among which number, he especially noteth Robert Hood, whome we now call Robyn Hood, and little John, who were famous theves. They continued in woodes, mountaynes and forestes, spoyling and robbing, namely such as were riche. Murders commonly they did none, except it were by the provocation of such as resisted them in their rifelynges and spoyles.

"And the sayde Maior sayth, that the aforesaid Robyn Hood had at his rule and commandment an hundred tall yomen, which were mightie men and exceeding good archers, and they were maintained by suche spoyles as came to their hands: and he sayth moreover, that those hundreth were such picked men, and of such force, that four hundreth men, whosoever they were, durst never set upon them. And one thing was commended in him, that he would suffer no woman to be oppressed, violated or otherwise abused. The poorer sort of people he favoured and would in nowise suffer their goodes to be touched or spoyled, but relieved and ayded them with such goodes as he gotte from the riche, which he spared not; namely the rich priests, fat abbotes, and the houses of riche earles. And although his theft and rapyn was to be contemned, yet the aforesayd aucthour prayseth him, and sayeth, that among the number of theeves, he was worthie the name of the most gentle theefe. . . . The sayd Robert Hood, being afterward troubled with sickness, came to a certain nunry in Yorkshire, called Berklies; where desirying to be let blood, he was betrayed and bled to death. After whose death, the prioresse of the same place caused him to be buried by the highway side, where he had used to rob and spoyle those that passed that way."

According to Dr. Gale, one-time Dean of York, Robin Hood died on the twenty-fourth of December, 1247, at the age of approximately eighty-seven. In Gale's papers was a copy of the inscription on Robin Hood's grave, which appeared in a History of Leeds. The lines have been called authentic by some and by others "ludicrous doggerel."

> *"Hear undernead dis latil stean*
> *Laiz Robert Earl of Huntingdon*
> *Nea arcir verza hie sa gevd*
> *An pipl kauld im Robin Heud*
> *Sick utlawz az hi an iz men*
> *Vil England nivr si agen*
> (OBIT 24 KAL DEKEMBRIS 1247)

Somehow the picture of Robin Hood becoming an earl of the realm is out of place, although most of the popular versions of the legend make him one of the nobility, either by birth or as a reward for his services to the kingdom. The bow was, and is, the weapon of everyone alike and it seems only fitting and proper to see the protagonist of yeoman archery remaining a simple woodsman, drawing ever to the head and ever sending his shafts dead into the gold, or into the forequarters of the king's deer. Novelists and script writers may make him an earl, and anthropologists may make him the middle-English earth sprite—equating him with Robin

Goodfellow—but to the archer he is ever the fairest bowmen of them all.

Apart from the romanticism of Robin Hood and his fellows, archery had become, by the thirteenth century, a recognized military arm of great importance to England. Royal statutes were passed saying that every male person not earning more than one hundred pence per year should be compelled to have in his possession a bow and arrows, along with other arms, both offensive and defensive. Going further, the laws made every man who had no possessions and no income, but who could still afford to purchase arms, the owner of a bow and sharp arrows. The arrows were to be blunt if the owner lived within the royal forests—apparently an early conservation measure. Officers were appointed by the Crown to see that all these weapons were in good order and ready for instant use. Edward I, under whom most of these laws came into being, brought Welsh archers into England, apparently to act as instructors, and used bodies of archers in his wars against the Scots. Archers were largely responsible for the English victory at Falkirk in these same wars.

Under Edward II, English archers were again used in the Border Wars and the king also sent archers to protect the Duchy of Aquitaine in France.

It was, however, under Edward III that archery reached its Occidental military peak. The Hundred Years' War—which actually lasted 116 years—began under this Edward. It was the Hundred Years' War that established England as a first-line military nation—through the strength of her bowmen. The causes and effects of the war are not the concern of this story; it is enough to say that large portions of France belonged to the Crown of England and Edward sought to establish his control over all of France. The net result was that all of Europe became involved in the war, which ultimately resulted in hundreds of far-reaching changes.

The actual beginning of the war came with the taking of the Island of Cadsand. Today the island is dry land, but in 1337 it was surrounded by water and was the property of Louis of Flanders. Flanders, to prove his devotion to Philip of France—Edward's adversary—fortified the little spit of land, and Edward seized on this as a cause for war. Under the Earl of Derby and Sir Walter de Manny, Edward dispatched a body of bowmen with orders to take and hold Cadsand. Froissart, the greatest historian of the era says, "The archers were ordered to draw their bows stiff and strong, and to set up their shouts; upon which those that guarded the haven were forced to retire, whether they would or not, for the first discharge did great mischief, and many were maimed and hurt." Archers had ushered in the long, long war.

Three years later, in 1340, the battle of Sluys was fought. It was an English victory which was to determine the course of the war for many years to come, although Edward failed to follow up the actual battle. It deserves special mention in the annals of archery, for although it was a sea battle, it was won by bowmen. Since it was a naval triumph, it won for Edward and his successors control of the English Channel and the sea for over a generation. Had England lost this control she would never have been in a position to supply Crécy, Poitiers and Agincourt, and the final outcome of the war would have been entirely different.

Early on the morning of June 22, 1340, the English fleet sailed out from Harwich and found the French lying in the harbor of Sluys. The English forces consisted of 147 ships, divided into three squadrons under the command of Sir Robert Morley, the Earl of Huntingdon and the Earl of Arundel. Facing them were 190 French ships carrying nearly thirty-five thousand men. But the French were handicapped in their command, which was split between two admirals, Hue Quieret and Pierre Behuchet, and a professional sea rover from Genoa, named Barbanero. Neither of the admirals seems to have been gifted with tactical genius, since they refused to leave the harbor and allowed Edward to stand at sea until wind, sun and tide were all in his favor. Instead, Quieret and Behuchet drew up their ships in three lines and anchored one wing of the forward line to the island of Cadsand. To insure the line against breaking, they then chained the ships together and prepared to withstand the English attack from a totally static position. Only Barbanero put out from the harbor with twenty-four galleys, to attack the English before they could sail into position.

Battle was joined when the first English line of ships, under Morley, swung into the harbor. Every third ship carried men-at-arms, while the other two were covered with bowmen. Trumpets sounded, drums rolled and even viols called, while the English shouted "St. George" and the French countered with their war cries. A hail of arrows whittled the French defenders down, and as soon as a ship bearing men-at-arms hit one of the French vessels, grapples went out and the men swarmed aboard to clean out what little resistance was left after the deadly volleys of arrows. Some of the arrows were especially made for sea fighting. Their heads were similar to those used by Commodus for ostrich shooting. But at Sluys they served another purpose, for the English bowmen, so armed, sought to cut the lines and rigging of the French ships with their half-moon blades The only refuge for the French lay in the shrouds and mizzentops, from which they poured down a rain of stones and other missiles on the boarders underneath.

One of the first vessels to fall to the English was the *Christopher,* which had recently been captured by the French in the Channel. Now speedily retaken, archers poured aboard and the ship put out to sea in pursuit of Barbanero and his galleys. In the meantime, French ship after French ship was taken by a combination of arrow fire and boarding parties. In one case the entire boarding party was stoned to death from above, but the battle went almost entirely in favor of the English. Seeing the defeat of his employers inevitable, Barbanero and his command fled from the fight, leaving the British in complete command of the scene. The first really great battle of the Hundred Years' War was won by sea-borne archers.

England was winning her spurs as a military nation, and at home the pressure made itself felt in a series of royal edicts, addressed to the sheriffs of the various counties. In 1342, Edward, looking forward to more battles abroad, ordered that every sheriff must provide five hundred white bowstaves and five hundred bundles of arrows for the coming war. The next year the order was repeated, with the additional demand that the sheriff of Gloucester was required to provide not only five hundred white bowstaves but five hundred painted staves as well.

The king also complained, by letter, to the sheriff of London about the condition into which archery had fallen. He said that skill with the bow was put aside in favor of useless sports and commanded that hereinafter the sheriff should see to it that such idle practices were abandoned and that leisure time upon holidays should be spent in the noble recreation of archery.

In 1342, Edward dispatched Sir Walter Manny to raise the siege of Hennebont. The castle was held by the Countess de Montfort against the combined armies of France, Normandy, Alençon and de Blois. With Manny were three hundred lances and a body of two thousand archers, who succeeded in relieving the gallant woman. But when Manny attempted to go farther into France, he was forced to retire from lack of food and supplies. Manny himself was not an archer, although he often led bowmen. Instead he favored the knightly pastimes of jousting and single combat, looking upon his yeomen as necessary but slightly uncouth.

At home, Edward was busy bringing together a standing army for use in the wars abroad. Under his grandfather and father, a system had been set up to raise troops, and Edward took full advantage of their example. Known as the Commissions of Array, the system was, in effect, a draft based on wealth. For example—any man who owned land or received rents to the amount of five pounds annually must provide the king with one archer. The commissioners did not care if the archer was the land owner or a man hired for the job. A land owner having an annual income of ten pounds must provide the king with one hobbler, who was either a mounted archer or a spearman. For a man with holdings of twenty-five pounds and upward, the provision was for a man-at-arms. The scale continued upward, so that the Earl of Oxford furnished twenty-three knights, thirty-four squires and sixty-three archers.

Under this Commission of Arrays, Edward mustered a force of approximately ten thousand men for use in the wars to come. A rough breakdown of the force shows there were about 3,700 archers; 3,500 Welsh, of whom over half were archers and the remainder spearmen; 2,700 hobblers, some of whom were also archers; and 1,200 men-at-arms. The remainder of the army was composed of miners and supernumeraries.

Edward's tactics grew out of a decisive battle fought in 1332 at Dupplin Muir. He also stole a page from the tactical plans of the Roman eunuch-general Narses, who originated this type of battle plan at Taginae in the year 552. Whether Edward realized that he was duplicating the Roman operation we cannot know, but he was well aware of the value of the lessons learned at Dupplin Muir.

Here, a fairly small body of men, headed by a group called "the Disinherited" met the combined Scottish forces of Donald, Earl of Mar. The Disinherited numbered about two thousand archers and five hundred knights, as opposed to the Scottish forces of twenty-two thousand men, mostly heavy cavalry. In the face of such odds, Baliol and Beaumont, the leaders of the Disinherited, chose a steep hill for their stand and dismounted all but fifty of the knights. The mounted men were placed in a solid phalanx, with the archers thrown out on either wing in a harrow formation. The heavily armored, dismounted knights were placed closest to the cavalry and there they awaited Mar's attack. Completely ignoring the archers, the Scottish forces plunged for the phalanx of cavalry, which buckled at their approach. The archers turned in on the attackers, subjecting them to such a deadly fire that they were completely routed. Beaumont then remounted the knights and pursued the survivors from the field.

Edward and his successors realized the efficiency of this harrow formation in battle and used it with great success in the great battles fought in France where the bowmen were used.

At Crécy the troops were drawn into three battles. The center, which was actually the rear, was directly under the command of the king and consisted of seven hundred men-at-arms and twelve hundred archers. The right battle was commanded by the Prince of Wales and was composed of some eight hundred men-at-arms, two thousand archers and one thousand Welsh. The left battle, under Northampton and the Earl of Arundel, was considerably weaker, having only eight hundred men-at-arms and twelve hundred archers. In both the right and left battles the archers were thrown forward in the now familiar harrow and protected on the front by shallow trenches and sharp pointed stakes driven into the ground at an angle. Although without armor, the lightly clad archers had no fear of attack except from fully armored knights, and they trusted to the stakes and trenches to protect them, should the French succeed in approaching their lines.

This total battle array was considerably weaker than the original body of ten thousand raised by Edward, but it must be remembered that he had fought several minor battles prior to Crécy. The accounts which credit Edward with over twenty-five thousand troops on the field to meet some one hundred thousand French must be considered wishful think-ing. More probably Edward faced approximately twelve thou-sand French and their allies, with a force of close to seventy-five hundred men, nearly two-thirds of whom were bowmen.

The comparatively few English had been engaged in a running campaign, closely pursued by the French. Edward chose his position well and had his lines in place, the trenches dug and the stakes in the ground long before the French arrived. The time was then late afternoon on the twenty-sixth of August, 1346. The King of France, seeing the disposition of the English, prepared to camp for the night in order to allow his men to come into some approxi-mation of battle order.

Unfortunately, there was so much disorder in the French ranks that the rear refused to stop until they were as far advanced as the van, and continued forward. The net result was total confusion in which bodies of men were shunted about needlessly and purposelessly. In the actual front of the French troops was a large body of Genoese crossbowmen, whose job it was to put the English archers out of combat. At five-thirty a sudden thunderstorm came up, completely soaking both sides, but the Genoese suffered more, since their bowstrings had not been waterproofed.

The English bows and bowstrings were well protected so that the rain did not interfere with their efficiency. As the Genoese advanced, shouting battle cries, the English re-mained in position, silent and with arrows in hand. Even the crossbow quarrels falling among them did not break the stillness of the line. Then on the signal they loosed a heavy fire of arrows into the ranks of the enemy.

The Genoese were badly hurt, and those left unwounded hastily retreated, cutting their useless strings as they ran. Again misfortune followed the French, for the crossbowmen came in between the advancing cavalry of the Earl of Alençon and the English. Enraged by the apparent defec-tion of the Italian mercenaries, Alençon and his men rode directly over them, adding even more confusion to the French lines.

The first attack, by the Genoese, had come at six o'clock and the English stood their ground until well after dark. During that time they repelled, by arrow fire, seventeen charges by French knights and men-at-arms without ever breaking ranks. Only a few of the Welsh, armed with long knives, slipped out onto the field to administer the coup de grâce to fallen enemies and to collect a few purses. At one time the right battle, under the Black Prince, seemed threatened but the situation was saved by a timely sweep across of the left, under Northampton and Arundel. One chronicler, speaking of the devastation wrought by the English arrows, says, ". . . Our archery was such, that the arrows, flying in the air as thick as snow, with a terrible noise, much like a tempestuous wind preceding a tempest, they did leave no disarmed place of horse or man unstricken." It must be remembered that not only were the ranks of bowmen steadfast in the battle, but the average man in the line was a qualified marksman, so that although the heavy fire was by volley, it had a doubly crippling effect due to its accuracy.

The casualties given for Crécy vary and no one set of figures seems at all reliable. According to one source there were nearly twelve hundred French dead and less than one hundred English, most of those Welsh, who were "cout out" with their long knives. Andrews, in his *History of Great Britain,* claims that three knights, one squire and a handful of men-at-arms and archers were lost. Still another accounting says that the French lost "the king of Bohemia, eleven other princes, eighty bannerets, twelve hundred knights, one thousand five hundred of the noblesse, four thousand men-at-arms and thirty thousand privates of the army, . . . left on the field of battle." If we agree that the French and their allies numbered only about twelve thousand in all, it is hard to reconcile this last account with reality. However, the fact remains that Crécy demonstrated to France and the world, the efficiency of the English longbow and the English yeoman. England had once and for all established her reputation as a nation of warriors and Crécy formed the moral beginning of the Hundred Years' War.

The second of the great bow-won battles occurred ten years later, when the Prince of Wales defeated the French at the Battle of Poitiers. In September 1356, the prince, in command of less than ten thousand men, met and defeated the French under King John, capturing him and his son. Sir John Smith, in his valuable *Discourse of the Weapons of War* claims that the French numbered sixty thousand, with ten thousand men-at-arms and thirty thousand horse.

The English operations which immediately preceded Poitiers were, in effect, nothing but a series of plundering raids. Ostensibly set in motion to protect English claims on the Duchy of Aquitaine, the forces took great care to avoid any lengthy sieges and were content to "hit and run." When the French army offered to give battle, the English were in an extremely poor position—overloaded with booty and spoils but perilously short of food. Had King John contented himself with holding the English in position, they would have been forced to surrender through hunger within a matter of days. The English compelled the French to attack, however, by feigning a retreat in the early morning and then falling back into prepared positions.

Unable to use really advantageous terrain, the English deployed on a long front, protected by heavy hedgerows. At the center the rows broke away, affording entrance to the English camp. Moreover, if the French and their German allies could gain this gap, they could then turn to either side and strike the unprotected archers from the rear. To prevent this, the Black Prince scattered men-at-arms and dismounted hobblers through the ranks of bowmen, but saved his heaviest concentration of armored men to protect the vital gap.

John of France, remembering the bitter defeat of Crécy, assumed that the English superiority lay in infantry and accordingly dismounted most of his men. The Germans serving under his banner refused to fight on foot, claiming that to do so would be an insult to their chivalric dignity. In addition, John kept three hundred knights for his first wave of attack, pinning his hopes on their ability to force through the English center.

The attack should have worked according to John's plan, with the initial shock provided by the three hundred French knights, the flower of the Gallic army. In the resulting melee, John felt his dismounted men would be able to wipe out any further English resistance. Acting on an age-old cavalry principle, John held in reserve one final body of armed men to deliver the coup de grâce, should it be needed.

The English were in this instance outnumbered by odds of six to one, but confidence in the longbow and in their leader held them firm in the hedgerows. Up and down the lines bowyers and fletchers moved, mending arrows and strings, selling spare shafts and heads and offering advice. Rations were already so short that half the men had had no breakfast, so they joked among themselves about the food to be had in the French camp.

When the three hundred knights charged, the English archers held their fire until the riders were well within range of the deadly arrows. Flamboyant courage and gallantry were not enough to survive the hail of arrows which flew out of the silent green hedges. Horses dropped or stumbled, pitching the mailed riders in grotesque heaps. Here and there a figure broke through the welter of fallen men and horses only to drop before he could reach the hedges.

There was little respite for the bowmen. As the last of the French knights fell, or was hacked down by the waiting men-at-arms, the Germans thundered at the hedgerows. Arrow fire was now constant, each archer loosing as he marked his target. The droning of massed arrows was replaced by single whirs as individual shafts found their marks. Wounded horses screamed at the arrows in their bodies and battling men grunted with each swordthrust. A few surviving Germans wheeled left and right, galloping back to join the French reserve.

Out on the plain, coming at the English position, the long iron line of French moved slowly. To the waiting bowmen it seemed a snail's pace. At different points along the line, men rushed out to the mass of fallen French and Germans, pulling arrows out with both hands. Food was not the only thing in short supply now; repelling two cavalry charges had sorely depleted the stock of arrows. The ranks of archers were thinner too; not all the horsemen had died on the plain —some had reached the hedges to wreak havoc before they were hacked down by the hobblers and men-at-arms.

King John's assessment of the situation showed clearly that he had little or no concept of missile warfare. The mere fact of dismounting his troops by no means rendered them invincible. Instead, it slowed them to a shuffling walk, while the archers picked and chose their targets from along the enemy's line. Frenchmen died by the tens, the twenties, the hundreds, and where they fell, other men filled the gaps. Archers searched frantically around them for more arrows, and finding none, reached for any weapon. The tide of battle had turned in favor of the French, in spite of John's stupidity. What was left of the French line moved on like some sword-wielding juggernaut. Deadly as the arrow fire had been, its volume had now slackened to the point where the French moved on, almost without loss.

Then the Black Prince sprang his trap and proved his ability as a general. Far to the rear, the final ranks of French cavalry were mustering to the attack. The main body was at hand grips with the hated English archers and men-at-arms. Suddenly English and Gascon horse under the Captal de Buche, Edward's captain of cavalry, swarmed into and through the French knights. Scarcely pausing, they rode at top speed down on the French infantry. What minutes before had seemed an English rout was now an overwhelming

English victory and the French laid down their arms, en masse. Smith claims in his *Discourse* that in addition to the King of France and his son, the English captured so many prisoners that their number exceeded that of their captors.

The Hundred Years' War dragged on, with both sides suffering severe losses in men and material. France was the heaviest hit, since it was on French soil that the majority of the actual battles were fought. Even when the French ventured overseas, they lost.

In the year 1377, the French landed a considerable body of troops on the Isle of Wight. The invaders took and razed the city of Franche-Ville and then, splitting in two colums, made for the fortress of Carisbrooke. The first section, ambushed by English archers, was completely wiped out, and the second was so sorely beaten, again by bowmen, at the castle that the French were forced to retreat from the island, leaving it in English hands.

At this time Richard II was King of England and records show that he maintained a standing bodyguard of archers, some authorities placing their number as high as four thousand. Once trouble arose in London, and the bodyguard, fearing for the king's life, drew their arrows and ranked themselves outside Parliament, to the terror of the people of the city. Holinshed, in his *Chronicle,* reports that the Genoese made an appeal to the king for assistance and that Richard replied by sending a body of archers to Genoa. There they sailed for the coast of North Africa and served with the Genoese in their campaigns against the Barbary Moslems.

Searching back for a picture of the bowmen of that era, we can find no better than that which appears in the pages of the *Canterbury Tales.* Geoffrey Chaucer shows us the archer:

> *"And he was clad in cote and hood of grene;*
> *A sheef of pecok-arowes brighte and kene*

Under his belt he bar ful thriftily;
(Wel coude he dresse his takel yemanly:
His arowes drouped nought with fetheres lowe,)
And in his hand he bar a mighty bowe;
A not-heed hadde he, with a broun visage.
Of wodecraft mel coude he al the usage.
Upon his arm he bar a gaye bracer,
And by his syde a swerd and a bokeler,
And on that other syde a gaye daggere,
Harneised wel, and sharp as point of spere;
A Cristofre on his brest of silver shene.
An horn he bar, the bandrik was of grene."

This, then, was the well-to-do yeoman of England, in the accouterments of war. Many, however, springing from every shire, were not so well off and could not afford the luxuries of a sword and buckler, but depended entirely on the longbow and perhaps a sheath knife. Nor did every man go with his arrows fletched with peacock feathers. As a matter of fact, the "gray goose feather" was much better thought of, for endurance, accuracy and reliability.

Part of the Hundred Years' War was fought by the English against their hereditary enemies the Scots. The clans, who resented English claims to their lands, found themselves allied constantly with the French and proved a stiff thorn in the backs of the English.

In 1402, the Earl of Douglas, commanding the Scottish army, met the English, under Lord Percy, at Halidownehill. Douglas soon learned the foolhardiness of attacking English archers. Enraged to see his pikemen and claymore-armed clansmen falling before the arrows, he went into battle accompanied by eighty fully armored knights. Douglas felt completely safe, since it was said that his armor had been three years in the making and was the finest obtainable. In the onslaught, Earl Douglas' armor was pierced by English shafts five times, and the Earl was captured, while the eighty knights with him were all killed or taken prisoner.

Time and again in widely separated battles the superiority of the English was apparent. The French depended on their men-at-arms and the Scots on pikemen, but neither type of fighter could make contact with the archer, or face up to his fire power. In addition the French were slow to abandon their faith in the invulnerability of the knight. While adhering blindly to the now-outmoded code of chivalry, they ignored or, at the most, condescended to common soldiery, as represented by their own men-at-arms and the English bowmen. The rapidity and accuracy of the English shooting was in effect heavy missile fire, which kept the enemy at a distance and so reduced his numbers that even when contact was established, the English men-at-arms and knights were in numerically superior position. Little wonder then that men like Sir John Fortesque said, "The might of the realme of England standyth upon archers."

The last of the great battles won by archers came in the year 1415, at Agincourt. Again an English king had invaded France in the hopes of making good his claim to that country. The odds were heavily against Henry the Fifth, with his body of some six thousand men, as they left the French city of Harfleur. Food was short, and his ranks were depleted by disease as well as hunger. What little food there was, was rotten or moldy at best.

Marching in three parallel lines, the archers moved through France, their flanks protected by horse. Behind them came the French army and ahead other bodies of troops were gathering to bar the way. So perilous was the English situation that some historians have called it a slow retreat. At last Henry gave the order to camp, since his men were incapable of going farther into armed and hostile country, while to turn back into the arms of the enemy was equally impossible. Camp was made on the outskirts of the village of Agincourt, on the night of October twenty-fourth, while Henry and his advisers chose their battle order. Using a slight slope, protected on either side by underbrush and woods, the English lines were drawn up. Close on their heels the French followed and camped so closely that sound carried from one camp to the other throughout the night.

Figures for the French forces range from one hundred thousand to 140,000 but a more accurate estimate shows them with from eighty to eighty-five thousand men in the field. Against these overwhelming odds, Henry lined up his six thousand archers so that they commanded the whole of the slight slope below them. As an added trick, under cover of night he sent a small force of picked archer marksmen down into a thick and thorny swamp which lay at the bottom of the hill and on the flank of the probable line of French advance. The rest of his bowmen were in the by now traditional harrow and also stationed so as to reinforce his center. In front of each archer the long stakes were driven, again to hold off any cavalry attack which might break through the curtain of arrow fire. In this instance the stakes were tipped at either end with iron, so that they would drive into the ground more easily, and not, as some writers have supposed, to cause worse injuries to the horses.

At dawn the armies marshaled themselves for battle. The French, under the command of the marshal D'Albert drew themselves up in close order at the foot of the hill facing the English, in a compact mass. In retrospect it is hard to imagine a more foolhardy battle order. First, by so placing his troops, D'Albert gave the English such a large target that the veriest tyro with a bow could hardly have missed it, even in the heat of battle. Secondly, such a mass, by its own unwieldiness, nullified in large part the overwhelming numerical superiority of the French, since fresh troops could not be brought up in haste. If the first attack failed, it would be necessary for subsequent movements to wait until the survivors had cleared the ground. D'Albert, unable to grasp the lessons of Crécy and Poitiers and with what now seems a typical French disregard for reality, staked his entire lot on the success of his first assault.

Henry rode up and down the lines of English archers, exhorting his men. Many of them were so sick with dysentery that they went into battle that day naked from the waist down, yet still determined to uphold the honor of England and the bow. Their king had warned them that if captured they would face the loss of their string fingers. France lived in terror of the bowmen and such a punishment seemed fitting to them. What the yeomen thought, standing that morning, is not recorded.

Hours passed while the two armies faced each other. Here and there in the English lines a man would stoop to pull short bits of grass, which he let fall to test the wind. In the French camp trumpets sounded and the steady roll of drums beat on the air. The waiting English could hear the neighing of horses and the clanging of armor as the knights mounted, but there were no signs of the French attack.

By nine o'clock Henry had begun to worry, fearing lest the French, having analyzed his weakness, were preparing to launch an attack from the rear. He dispatched mounted scouts to screen him from behind and then, shortly before ten, ordered the trumpets to sound the attack. At the sound, every archer knelt and kissed the ground before him, then sprang to his feet and began the serious business of fighting.

D'Albert had been waiting for Henry to make the first move, and the instant the English trumpets sounded gave the orders for the French to advance. A mass of men and horses thundered into line and charged straight at the archers, across the bottom of the valley and then up the slope. They rode without hope, for all their courage; rode straight into the rain of arrows. A prearranged signal brought the marksmen in the swamp into the fray and this flanking attack completed the rout of the first French attack. The survivors broke and, turning, rode full into the mass of their own lines.

The confusion which followed took some little time and while the French sorted themselves out, the English calmly and carefully continued to shoot at their enemies. At last the second wave took form out of the mass, and under the banner of the Duke D'Alençon attacked the hill again. Once more the arrows hummed and struck, once more men and horses toppled, but this time the French had a slight advantage. Because the English had not advanced, they had had no opportunity to replenish their supply of arrows. Their fire, therefore, was not as heavy as it had been during the first attack, so that more French broke through, reaching for the stakes. To compensate for this, when the French came close enough, the forward ranks of bowmen put down their weapons and grasping short swords or battle-axes, went into hand-to-hand combat. Henry threw out cavalry from either side, driving the French back down the slope. This second wave of attack was the turning point of the battle and when it was repulsed the French spirit was broken so that England's victory was clear.

In spite of the triple victories of Crécy, Poitiers and Agincourt, archery as a weapon of war was on the downgrade. It is believed that Edward III was using a very primitive form of cannon at Sluys and the introduction of gunpowder, no matter what its exact date, was the beginning of the end for the archer soldier. Over four hundred years were to pass before the bow and arrow were overcome by rapid-fire from a gun, but the seeds were sown in the fourteenth century.

As guns and gunpowder became more and more common, the use of the bow gradually died out, and in some instances it was not the gun but the crossbow which served to displace the longbow. Under Henry VII of England a royal order was issued in which the use of the crossbow was officially forbidden under penalty of fining and imprisonment.

For the kings at least recognized the value of the longbow as a weapon. But the factor of human inertia is a hard thing to overcome, even by royal decree. The making of a skillful archer is a matter of years, the making of a skillful cross-bowman or an adequate gunner is but a matter of months. It was far too easy to attain a certain amount of proficiency with the other weapons for the bow to remain highly popular.

We must not, however, suppose that archery died over-night, following Agincourt. Far from it—we read instead that "in Henry VI's time, John, Lord Bellay, being accompanied with two hundred lances at the least, met by chance with an English captain, called Berry, who had to the number of eighty archers. Perceiving the Frenchmen, he presently re-duced his men into a hearse or harrow, turning their backs to a hedge, that the lances might only charge them in front; and giving their vollies of arrows at the French lances charging, did so wound and kill men and horse, that they overthrew them, slew many and took divers of them prisoners . . . . And within a while after that, a French captain, Cuion de Coing, accompanied by 120 lances, went out to seek an adventure with the English and was met with Sir William Olde, with sixteen or twenty archers on horseback, who dis-mounted and formed in a broad way, whence the lances could not charge them but in front: and the French charging them, the vollies of arrows of these few archers, wrought such notable effect against the French horsemen, that they broke and overthrew them in such sort, that there were divers of the French slain, and many taken prisoners." Again, the same author, Sir John Smith, says, "This en-gagement doth evidently shew the great excellence of arch-ery, against all other sorts of weapons; in which battle of Herrings, Sir John Falstaff, with other brave English cap-tains, by the grace of God, and terrible shot of arrows, over-threw the bastard of Orléans, the lord high constable of Scotland, the Count of Claremont, with many other captains of great account, and their whole army of Frenchmen and

Scots, in which there were a great number of French harquebussiers and crossbowmen, which against the archers wrought no effect."

Smith was such an advocate of archery that his enthusiasms often led him into hot water. His work, the *Discourses* appeared in 1590, and was in effect a wholesale condemnation of the new weapons "the mosquet and caliver" and the harquebus. The book was hastily repressed by English military authorities and within three weeks of its publication, copies were no longer available. His was the stern voice, crying for a return to the older and more effective ways of the longbow.

Obviously both the early guns and crossbows remained rather hopelessly outclassed by the skill and rapid fire of the archers. Indeed, when James I, the King of Scotland, was confined in England, he was so impressed with the longbow and its use that on his return to Scotland he caused a law to be passed by the Scottish Parliament in 1424.

"That all men might busk thame to be archares, fra they be twelve years of age: and that at ilk ten pounds' worth of land, thair be made bow markes, and specialle near paroche kirks, quhairn upon halie days men may cum, and at the leist schute thrusye about, and have usye of archarie; and whassa usis not archarie, the laird of the land sall rais of him a wedder, and giff the laird raisis not the said pane, the king's shiref or his ministers sall rais it to the king."

In England, Edward IV proclaimed that every Englishman and Irishman living in England must have, of his own, a bow of his own height, "to be made of yew, wych, or hazel, ash or auborne or any other reasonable tree, according to their power." The same law provides that butts or mounds of earth for use as marks must be erected in every town and village and listed a series of penalties for those who did not practice with the longbow.

Richard III was one of the kings who recognized the value of archery, and Shakespeare makes him say, just prior to the battle of Bosworth Field, "Draw, archers, draw your arrows to the head." There are also records of Richard's having sent a body of one thousand archers to France to aid the Duke of Brittany. Henry VII, whose anti-crossbow legislation we have already noted, also sent large levies of English archers to fight for the Duke of Brittany. During this entire period English longbowmen served in many parts of the then-known world.

A rather interesting fragment concerning these periods of overseas service has come to us through Washington Irving. The novelist translated the Spanish *Chronicles of the Conquest of Granada* and speaks of English archers serving in the wars against the Moors in Spain. The Earl of Rivers, who had distinguished himself on the Tudor side at Bosworth Field, left England that same year and went to Spain, with a company of knights, men-at-arms and archers. "He brought with him a hundred archers, all dexterous with the long-bow and the clothe-yard arrows; also two hundred yeomen, armed cap-a-pie, who fought with pike and battle-ax; men robust of frame and of prodigious strength." These sturdy men of the shires, so far from home, found themselves often at odds with their allies and the Spanish soldiers seem to have feared, but respected them. A friar, Padre Fray Antonio Agapida, says of them in the *Chronicles,* "They were often noisy and unruly . . . in their wassail . . . and their quarter of the camp was prone to be a scene of loud revel and sudden brawl . . . their pride was silent and contumelious . . . they yet believed themselves the most perfect men upon earth . . . it must be said of them, that they were marvellous good men in the field, dexterous archers . . . they did not rush forward fiercely, nor make a brilliant onset, like the Moorish or Spanish troops, but they went into the fight deliberately, and persisted obstinately and were slow to find out when they were beaten. . . . Withal they were much esteemed, yet little liked by our soldiery, who considered them staunch companions in the field, yet coveted but little fellowship with them in the camp. . . . Often they did practice with their great bows . . . sending the arrows unerringly to any mark set of them."

Later the *Chronicles* mentions the first battle in which the English took part, saying, "Lord Rivers . . . was merely armed *en blanco,* that is to say, with morion, backpiece and breastplate; his sword was girded by his side and in his hand he wielded a powerful battle-ax. He was followed by a body of his yeomen, armed in like manner and by a band of archers, with bows made of the tough English yew tree . . . they soon made their way into the midst of the enemy, but when engaged in the hottest of the fighting they made no shouts or outcries. . . . They pressed steadily forward, dealing their blows and cutting their way with their battle-axes, like woodmen in the forest; while the archers, pressing into the opening they made, plied their bows vigorously and spread death and destruction on every side." The *Chronicles* seems wrong in listing the bows as being made of "the English yew trees." What the English bows were made of we do not know, but if it was yew, then it had probably been imported and possibly from Spain itself. For Spain at one time had supplied England with many of her rough yew bowstaves. Spain too had suffered raids by English bowmen under the Black Prince. Spanish pride was so affronted at this that legends say all yew trees were cut down after the invasion and allowed to grow no more for fear the English would come again, plying Spanish yew bows.

The importation of good wood for use as bows had been a sore subject with the English many times, and under Richard III a law was passed which complained of the mendacity of Lombard traders, who had caused inflation in the price of imported yew staves. Formerly a hundred staves had brought two pounds, but due to the machinations of the traders, the price had risen to eight pounds. To counteract this inflation of a much-needed article, the Act provided that for every butt of wine imported by the traders, they must also bring in a bundle of ten bowstaves, or face a heavy fine. During the rule of Henry VIII there are other statutes recorded to bring down the price of bowstaves, for seemingly inflation was again current among the bowyers.

The reign of Henry VIII is closely associated with archery, in spite of the fact that as a military weapon the bow was steadily losing stature. The Merry Monarch was himself an archer of no little ability and we find instance after instance where he tried to instill in his subjects the old love of the bow. To aid him came the voice of the church, in the person of Bishop Latimer. This worthy, preaching before the king, and with obvious royal approval, has left us with perhaps the only sermon praising and upholding archery.

"The art of shutynge hath ben in times past much estemmed in this realme; it is a gyft of God, that he hath given us to excell all other nations withal. It hath ben Goddes instrumente whereby he hath given us manye victories agayneste our enemyes. But now were have taken up horynge in townes, instead of shutynge in the fyldes. A wondrous thynge, that so excelente a gyft of God shoulde be so little esteemed. I desire you, my lordes, even as you love honoure, and glorye of God, and intende to remove his indignacion, let there be sente furth some proclimacion, some sharpe proclimacion to the justices of peace, for they do not theyr dutye. Justices now be no justices; there by many good actes made for thys matter already. Charge them upon their allegiance, that this singular benefit of God may be practised; and that it be turned not into bollyng, and glossyng and horyng, within the townes; for they be negligente in executyng the lawes of shutynge. In my tyme, my poore father was so diligent to teach me to shute, as to learne any other thynge; and so I think other menne dyd thyr children. He taught me how to draw, howe to lay my bodye in my bowe, and not to draw with strength of armes, as other nacions do, but wyth strength of bodye. I had my bowes bought me according to my age and strength; as I increased in them, so

my bowes were made bigger and bigger: for men shall never
shute well, excepte they be brought up in it. It is a goodly
arte, a holesome kind of exercise and much commended in
phisike. Marcilius Sicinus, in hys boke de triplica vita (it
is a greate while sins I red hym nowe) but I remember he
commendeth thys kynde of exercise and sayth, that it
wrestleth agaynste many kyndes of diseases. In the rever-
ence of God, let it be continued. Let a proclimacion go furth,
charging the justices of peace, that they see such actes and
statutes kept as were made for thys purpose."

Reading these lines, one can sense the sincerity of Latimer's
feelings, but such fulminations were only temporarily effective and they could not stem the tide which flowed away
from archery. Then Henry the king, to further bolster his
favorite sport, instituted another decree to prevent more de-
cay in archery. Under its ruling all men under the age of
sixty, with the exception of clergymen, justices and certain
other privileged professions, must use the longbow and
have both a bow and a good supply of arrows available for
instant use. Secondly, every person who had a son or sons
between the ages of seven and thirteen must provide each
of them with a suitable bow and two arrows. Moreover, if
any father or master of menservants of the age of seventeen,
permitted them to be without a bow and four arrows for
a period of one month, the said master or father, must pay
six shillings, and eight pence for each and every offense.
After that age each servant or free youth must provide his
own bow and arrows up until such time as he became sixty,
at the risk of the same fine. The edict also provided again
for the erection of butts and targets in every city, town and
hamlet and ordered the inhabitants thereof to practice
there on all holidays and "at every other convenient time."

The Merry Monarch's efforts to revive archery were certainly well meant, but time and gunpowder were no friends
to Henry Tudor. In all fairness it must be noted that in the
year 1510 the king sent to North Africa a body of fifteen

hundred bowmen from the shires. They were sent at the request of Ferdinand of Spain, who, having driven the Moors from Spain, now sought to push them out of their ancestral home in Africa. But the bow, as the primary English weapon, was rapidly becoming passé. When England stood to arms to repel the Spanish Armada a few years later, less than fifty percent of the mustering levies were bowmen, although the men of Buckinghamshire and Oxfordshire still clung almost exclusively to the old weapon.

The first really great archery writer appeared on the English scene during the reign of Elizabeth the First. John Smith's approach to the subject had been a limited one, with all his emphasis resting on the military value of the bow in comparison with any of the other then-current arms. But Roger Ascham, who served as a tutor to Elizabeth when she was still a princess, was the author of the book *Toxophilus,* which remains the classic in the field. Allowing for certain minor differences in phraseology and certain advances which have been made in equipment, Ascham's book is as valuable to the archer today as when it was written four centuries ago. His "Instructions" can be, and are, used today in teaching many of our neophyte archers. We can truthfully say that Aschams relationship to the bow corresponds to that of Isaac Walton's to the rod and reel.

The fact that archery had lost its pre-eminence in the field of war did not mean, however, that it was not popular. Today we feel archery is rapidly gaining ground as a sport, but we still cannot call up as many archer sportsmen as did the English in the year 1583. Then, in a section of London known as Shoreditch, a two-day meeting attracted three thousand active participants, who shot from daybreak until it was too late to see the targets. Elizabeth had honored the archers of the realm by composing her bodyguard from among strapping young bowmen, and the bow continued to hold its place in ritual.

During the time of Charles the Second, archery competi-

tion caused a traffic holdup in London and a general breakdown of military morale. Four hundred archers were com-
peting in Hyde Park, and thousands of people thronged
along the edge of the grass to watch. One of the feature
attractions of that meet was the shooting of a round by all
contestants, using whistling arrows. When these shafts began
to scream their way to the targets, the noise attracted the attention of three regiments of infantry who were drilling in
a nearby section of the park. The men became so engrossed in
watching the archers that they laid down their arms and remained for the rest of the day, cheering the marksmen.

Archery remained dear to the hearts of the English for
many years and the people in general looked on top-scoring
bowmen with the same affection and pride which is now ac-
corded to football players and home-run kings. One of the
most pointless treason trials of all times came about through
this same adoration.

One John King of Hipperholme in Yorkshire was, in his
day, the best archer in the whole of the north of England.
It was, however, King's misfortune to reach the zenith of
his shooting during the time when Oliver Cromwell was
ruling England with a stern and puritanical hand—constantly fearful of rebellion by loyalist forces.

King defended his laurels against all comers one day and
defeated them all smartly. The records fail to show how
many golds he scored, but the Yorkshire people were properly appreciative and, hoisting the winner on their shoulders, carried him about the town with cries of "a King," "a
King." Cromwell's men, mistaking their jubilation for signs
of incipient revolt, promptly dispersed the crowd and
placed the "King" under arrest. Shortly thereafter John
King was carried to the city of Manchester and there stood
trial for the crime of high treason against the state. Fortunately, even Roundhead justice could be tempered, and
amid cheering crowds the "King" of the archers was freed.

In the late 1700's, Sir Ashton Lever and his friends formed

the Toxophilite Society, which is still in existence. Now called the Royal Toxophilite Society, or more informally "The Royal Tox," it served for many years to keep the spirit of archery alive in England and by, extension, served as the foster father for the sport in the United States. Without the work of the "Tox" and a few other societies, it might well be that archery would not have survived as a sport. For although the American Indian played and plays a large part in the imagination of children everywhere, it was not from the tradition of the "noble savage" that American archery had its roots, but rather from the memories of shooting in Merrie England.

One last anecdote, however, before leaving England. It concerns the last recorded use of the bow as an offensive weapon in the British Isles. In the year 1791, in the city of Edinburgh, two gentlemen argued over some obscure point and, failing to come to an agreement, resolved to settle their affairs by means of a duel. The gentleman challenged, availing himself of his rights, named the bow and three arrows apiece as the weapons. Properly seconded and with a surgeon in attendance, the two made their way outside the city on the following morning and took their shots. Each man stood firm at one hundred paces and shot full for his opponent. Fortunately neither gentleman suffered the slightest injury, and the affair ended to the satisfaction of both parties, but one can imagine the shades of Crécy shaking their heads disdainfully.

8

The Red Archers

ANYONE WHO THINKS OF ARCHERY ALMOST AUTOMATICALLY
calls to mind either the American Indian closing in for the
kill with drawn shaft and war paint or Robin Hood stalking
the king's deer in Sherwood Forest.

Robin Hood, as we have said, existed, although it is doubtful if his admirers would recognize him in the flesh, so covered is he with the stuff of folklore. Certainly, too, the
Amerindian bowman existed but he was not an outstanding
archer, and to so credit the Indian is gilding the lily, to put
it mildly. The process of historical debunking is an unhappy
one since all too often it robs us of childhood idols and ideas;
but there is little if any evidence to show that the average
American Indian was more than a fair shot with his bow.
That fact should not, however, be allowed to obscure the
woodscraft, courage and resourcefulness of the red tribes. The
Indian was a patriot fighting for what he considered to be his
rights. If his methods were cruel, if in a few scattered instances his word was not his bond—remember that the white
man's side of the struggle was far from decent and honesty
played an extremely small role in our dealings with the Indian. We were the only ones to set a price for scalps.

At the coming of the white man, the Indian and his cousin
the Eskimo were well established on the two continents of
the Western Hemisphere. The Eskimo, probably the last to
arrive from Asia, occupied the northernmost reaches—the

170

land which is truly ice and snow. But at the timber line the Indians began, and they stopped only at Tierra del Fuego. In all that vast expanse of land there were literally thousands of tribes, with almost as many varying degrees of culture. Some were bestial, some had achieved a high degree of political sophistication, some lived in vast cities, while others were content with rude jacals or huts. Had they been allowed to advance along their own lines, they might have established civilizations as mighty and complex as anything the Old World had produced. As it is, archeologists, anthropologists and historians still shake their heads in awe and wonder at the tremendous advances made by the Mayas, the Aztecs and the Incas. Nor can we say that we know too much about these cultures; new discoveries, new methods, recording, translation and collation constantly add to our knowledge.

It is fairly safe to say that every Indian tribe had the bow in one form or another. Their use of the weapon varied— with tribal psychology and advancement, and with their territory—some areas were more suited to its use. But many tribes used other weapons in preference. For example, the Maya used the obsidian-edged sword and the throwing stick, which was called the atlatl. The latter was so universally used by them that it almost excluded the more effective bow. In the North the Eskimo used both bow and throwing stick, as the occasion demanded.

That the bow was almost universal in the two continents is not strange, if we subscribe to the theory that all the Indians of the Americas came originally from Asia by way of the Bering Straits. For many years this has been the most popular way to account for the existence of the many tribes. Cultural interlinkages go far to substantiate the claim, and until the exponents of the other schools—Phoenician, Atlantean, Akkadian, Polynesian—submit more conclusive evidence, it will remain the only really acceptable idea.

The throwing stick of the Maya has been offered as a stumbling block to the Asiatic-origin premise, but it need not necessarily be one. In the history of weapon development it would seem as though the throwing stick, in many cases, was the immediate predecessor of the bow, and often the two forms continued to be used by one culture, as in the case of the Eskimo. It is perfectly reasonable to suppose this to have been the case with the Mayas, and that as centuries passed they concentrated on the atlatl, to the exclusion of the bow. In the New Empire of the Mayas, where there was a considerable mixture of Toltec culture overlaid, the bow was more prominent, which would seem to indicate that the Mayas themselves had no active prejudice against the bow. Tribes to the north and the south of them used the bow, and any other interpretation of the data would lead to the assumption that the Mayas were either completely isolated, from a cultural standpoint, or that they represented a completely foreign intrusion which suddenly occurred in Central America.

The bow itself offered almost as many variations as there were tribes. Interestingly, the areas where a highly developed bow occurred are those which were in closest contact with Asiatic influences. Obviously this offers strong support for the theory of Asiatic origin and also leads one to the conclusion that the tribes did not come over all at one time but rather in a series of migrations. Thus, early waves would bring with them early forms of the bow, while later travelers would bring a more complex archery culture.

We are also tempted to theorize that all these tribal waves had ceased before the domestication of the horse in Asia. A primitive horse had been indigenous to this hemisphere but was long extinct when man appeared. The first horses, as we know them, arrived with the Spanish. The Indians were totally unfamiliar with the concept of riding. Even their racial memory, in the form of myth, provided them with no clue, so that they at first conceived of the horse and rider as one entity. Since the tribes which first tamed and rode the horse readily recognized its value, it is logical that had they possessed horses they would have brought their herds with them during an intercontinental migration.

To bolster up further the theory of successive waves, there are instances, particularly in South America, where there seems to have been a definite degenerative tendency in making archery equipment. For example, in regions of Amazonia, where it was formerly customary for stone arrowheads to be used, the tribes now use only hardened wood. Our consideration of this degenerative tendency must, however, be qualified by the knowledge that here, as in every primitive culture, such manufacture is in large part governed by the raw materials available.

Our contacts with the Indians, although in the majority of cases made under adverse conditions, allow us to draw a fairly complete picture of archery both before and after the coming of the white man. One rule, which obtains universally, is aptly demonstrated by a look at the many bow variants. One can always look to find the type of bow in use to be the one which is best adapted for the purpose which the archer has in view.

This rule is not confined to this hemisphere, but works under almost any set of circumstances. The fact that the English longbow was poorly designed in view of modern techniques and was wasteful of both materials and energy can hardly be described as proof of the reverse. While the longbow did not produce optimum results, it was, within its own frame of reference, ideally suited to its purposes. It is as unfair to compare the performance of the modern, engineer-designed, stress-tested weapon to the medieval longbow as it is to match the latter against the puny bow of the African pygmy. Each, in its own place and in its own time, performed those tasks which were necessary to its user.

This "best-adapted" type will invariably gain the mastery over other forms, supposing that the raw materials necessary for its construction are to be found on the spot, or within an area of accessibility, through either barter or capture. Thus flint and obsidian arrowheads would be found not only in those areas where the stones occur, but in regions where the stones could be obtained by barter or through the seizure of a source of supply. Deposits where flint was easily obtained were often the subject of constant conflict as tribe after tribe endeavored to seize and retain use of these valuable holdings.

Interestingly enough, scientific tests have proven that the Indian assessment of flint's value is quite correct. In a series of experiments, conducted under laboratory conditions, the late Saxton Pope proved conclusively that arrowheads made of flint have a far greater penetrating power than do metal heads of conventional pattern, due not to the material involved, but to the form which the stone takes in use. The natural conchoidal fracture of flint, and its cousin, chert, gives these heads an average of twenty-five percent more penetration. It is for this reason that some of our manufacturers are today marketing metal heads which are cast to imitate the characteristic contours of the flint heads.

Ethnologists often utilize the arms of primitive peoples for the purpose of mapping the extent of a given tribe or a series of linked tribes. But in so doing they must bear in mind that "pure" weapons are rare. If, for example, one tribe decorates the upper limb of the bow with a bunch of feathers, they cannot necessarily say that wherever this bow occurs, the tribe in question also occurs. For one thing, such bows, along with other weapons, would be legitimate trophies of war. Some tribes did not collect scalps but, rather, useful artifacts which served a double purpose—as tokens of victory and to specifically make the victor's life easier or richer. Another factor which must be taken into consideration when one formulates an ethnological map is that often one tribe would serve as the bowyers or fletchers for a whole series of people living around them. Or again, skilled craftsmen would work as flint nappers, who through proficiency in chipping came to occupy a highly respected position in several primitive societies.

Thirdly, we must remember that many Amerindian tribes practiced slavery—mostly in the form of taking war captives, whose servitude was tantamount to outright slavery. These slaves would often make weapons embodying their own tribal patterns so that methods of construction and decoration might be found far from their point of origin, without in any way indicating an actual tribal or cultural intrusion.

When the Amerindian way of life was interrupted by exploration, colonization and exploitation, the tribes were, almost without exception, hunters. In fact the entire population of North and South America, under the influences of its natural surroundings, was a conglomeration of nomadic hunters—and the greater portion of them adhered to this mode of life as long as it was feasible. Even the highly evolved Mayan and Incan civilizations were dependent on the hunters for meat, and we have but to look at the Plains Indians of the United States to realize the adherence to the practice. With the buffalo herds harried to the point of near extinction, the tribes were reduced to existing on a governmental dole of meat. And although some of these tribes have made a certain amount of adjustment, the great hunters remain largely as picturesque hangers-on, unable to adapt themselves to a life without hunting. There is, however, hope that the passage of time will make the tribes more amenable to this change. The tribes of the eastern seaboard, having been subject to white influences for a longer period, are better integrated into society as a whole. It is less than a hundred years since the subjugation of the western tribes and already some, like the erstwhile warlike Apache, have adopted a course which makes them nearly indistinguishable from their neighbors. Perhaps soon other tribes will succumb to the necessity of civilization, albeit with a subsequent loss of color and drama—both in their lives and ours.

In the more remote sections of Central and South America where there are still "wild" Indians, the economy is still geared to hunting, and when this is lacking or taken from them, they too become dependent on the generosity of governments.

Because their way of life was so bound to the hunt, the Indians invariably developed and utilized skills and methods which came close to precluding failure. For this reason and for this reason alone, the Indian became a magnificent stalker and an equally first-rate woodsman. He did not depend on his bow to bring down game at any great range, but rather, got so close to his target that the arrow simply became infallible. Being completely natural in his approach to these things, the primary thought in the mind of the Indian was to bring home the game—anything else was secondary. And if consummate skill in getting close to his game did not succeed, the Indian resorted to the use of arrow poisons.

South America provides us with the widest range of poisons which were used in conjunction with archery. Most of them were dependent, in the mind of the hunter, for their efficiency on the magico-religious ceremonies which surrounded their preparation. Curare is the active agent in a half dozen arrow poisons—but it is extremely doubtful if the hunter or the magician would be able to tell whether it was this, or some of the less toxic ingredients which acted as the killing agent. Or if a medicine man prepared a gourd full of decayed animal matter and menstrual blood, into which ray spines, which served as arrowheads, were dipped, he was sure it was his incantations which rendered the mixture effective. This positive belief in the effect of religious magic may be hard for us to understand, but it was a constant and all-powerful factor in the lives of the Amerindians, and any attempt to understand them must take it into full consideration.

All through the use of the bow by the tribes on both continents we find this element of magic playing an active part. The possession of an effective bow, with its complement of arrows, was often the sign that a youth had become a man, and in many tribes it was and is taboo for a woman to touch the apparatus of the full-fledged hunter. The penalty for an infraction of this restriction might even involve death, for the Indian believed that a bow touched by a woman would no longer be accurate, and with a lack of accuracy there was a lack of food—imperiling the entire sept or clan. Most of these prohibitions or taboos sprang from similar beliefs and were, as far as the Indian was concerned, vital to the continued well-being of himself and his family. To us many of them are strange and some seem so farfetched as to defy a ready analysis.

The Amerindians used what is called the "primary release" in shooting. This style of arrow release is also called the "pinch draw," since it involves drawing the arrow back, pinched between the thumb and the knuckle of the forefinger of the arrow hand. Most archers realize that this is one of the poorest draws, particularly for use with heavy bows. But the only concession which the Indian would make to this point was to thicken the nock end of the arrow shafts in some cases so that the thumb and forefinger would have a better grip against the pressure of the bowstring. While this modification will assist the archer to a certain extent, the primary release still falls far short of the efficiency of the Mediterranean or three-finger draw, which most archers use today. But the Indians carried their taboos even into the field of the draw. Among some of the cannibalistic tribes of South America, the Indians would refuse to eat the thumb and forefinger of the victim if he had been a warrior, since to do so would render him incapable of hunting in the after life. Quite to the contrary, other tribes felt that to eat the arms of a warrior lent to the eaters some part of his accuracy as an archer, in an example of what is called associative magic.

The degree of the taboo varied from tribe to tribe. Dr. Saxton Pope adopted a California Indian named Ishi, and he has noted several taboos which this man observed in connection with his archery tackle. First, the bow must always be unstrung when not in use. While Ishi made a taboo of this, many archers using self-bows will understand perfectly the reasoning behind it, for all too often a strung bow will "follow the string," that is, hold the strung shape even when not braced, with a resultant loss of cast. The second prohibition was one we have met before, namely that a woman must not touch the bow. The third consisted in refusing children the right to handle the bow and arrows. This may be simply because children might break the tackle, but a more probable reconstruction is that for an uninitiated individual— one who was not past puberty—to handle the bow would again result in a loss of accuracy. The final injunction was against anyone's stepping over the bow. Some authorities say that this was because a body passing over the bow would break its connection with the powers of the Sun and Sky, thereby rendering it ineffective.

However, Ishi told Pope that any of these taboos, once broken, could be atoned for by a ritual washing of the bow, first with water and then with sand. This removed the evil influences which had resulted from the broken laws and once more rendered the bow fit for use. In other tribes tackle which has become ritually unclean or useless must be destroyed and completely replaced in order to nullify the harmful influences resulting from the broken taboos.

An examination of Indian arrows in museums and private collections will readily prove that the Indian was not a great fletcher. Some of the shafts are brilliantly decorated, but the wood itself was often crooked and the arrowheads show that the maker's knowledge of pressure chipping in flint was rather rudimentary. White men can and do make far superior flint arrowheads. Feathers were set on the shaft in a variety of ways and with an equal variety of trimming, but it was seldom that any given set of "flights," as the individual feathers on an arrow are called, would match. Some tribes dispensed with feathers entirely and shot bare shafts. The most primitive arrows in the New World were made by Costa Rican Indians, who used neither feathers nor head on their shafts, but simply propelled a stick by means of the bow-string. In other tribes the feathers were sewn on, while some glued them to the wood. Little wonder, then, that in many cases a medicine man was called upon to pray and chant over the arrows of warriors about to go hunting or on the war trail.

The Eskimo followed similar customs, and one of the most colorful of their legends concerns the death of the last Viking chief in Greenland. The colonies of Norsemen had gradually been abandoned, and at last only one man and his household held out against the cold, the animals and the hostile Eskimo. He refused to leave in the face of this adversity until his Eskimo neighbors called in a famous shaman, or witch doctor, from far away on the mainland. The shaman chanted for three days and three nights over a single shaft, crying to the spirits to imbue it with the power to pierce the armor of the Norseman. When the ceremony was over, an Eskimo hunter took the now sacred arrow and crept within bowshot of the Viking house. There he waited until the white man came out. The bowstring twanged, the arrow sped through the cold, crisp air and the last of the Vikings pitched forward, with the shaft stuck like some grotesque twig in his throat.

We see nothing extraordinary in this, more than a killing shot by the Eskimo which resulted in the death of the last intruder. But to the primitive mind—Eskimo, Indian or Cro-Magnon—it represented the triumph of magic and religion over hitherto invincible power, which was equated with other, evil magic.

The standard of Eskimo equipment was higher than the average Indian equivalent. Their bows were composite, and they had a unique method of fixing feathers to their arrows. After the feathers were stripped, ready for attaching, the Eskimo fletcher would force the thin slice of quill into the wood of the shaft by means of tiny ivory blades, made especially for this purpose. Quivers were of seal skin and when hunting on the ice floes at sea, the men carried their bows in waterproof bow cases.

We can give two reasons for the fact that the Eskimo bows were composite in form. One is that as the last men across the land or ice bridge at the Bering Straits, they brought with them a highly advanced type of bow from their Siberian homeland. While this may be true, there is a much more likely explanation in that it was far easier, with the materials at hand, for the Eskimo to develop the composite independently. On the assumption that he on arrival was familiar with a self-bow, when he found himself in a land lacking in wood, it would seem probable that he would seek for the best substitute—and that a composite made of driftwood, horn and sinew would be the result. Among a series of native American bows tested, it was found that the Eskimo and the Alaskan Indian were of the heaviest draw, both pulling to about eighty pounds. However the Eskimo bow proved under test conditions to have a maximum flight twenty yards greater than that of the Alaskan Indian specimen. The Eskimo bow shot a distance of two hundred yards, while the Indian could not attain more than 180 yards.

While maximum cast and shaft penetration are closely linked, we will assume that the Eskimo sought for the former, rather than the latter. His hunting territory was all in the open, where the factor of additional yardage would be vitally important—might well spell the difference between eating and starvation. The Alaskan Indian, however, living below the tree line, found that maximum cast was not so essential as close range power and penetration—to kill moose, caribou and big bear. Therefore, in heavily wooded country his design resulted in a bow capable of killing the largest animals on the continent, at what he considered a reasonable range. The two bows, developing almost side by side and closely matched, show the validity of the principle stated previously, that the bow type which is the best adapted for the purpose will always gain the mastery.

The adaptability of the Indian himself is an interesting subject. While generalization, particularly on such a complex topic, is always dangerous, it has been said that in most instances the North American Indian was more gifted in that respect than his South American counterpart. To illustrate the point let us examine the impact of the white man on two widely separated groups of tribes—those of the great central plains of the United States and those of the rolling pampas of Argentina and Paraguay.

Both of these groups were without horses until the animals were brought in by soliders and colonists. A few horses escaping from the Spanish herds in both North and South America rapidly produced a large body of wild stock. The Indian, by then familiar with the custom of riding, learned the art with a facility and ease that was surprising. Thus within a few years after the first Spanish invasion of the territories involved, the native populations had developed into expert horsemen and had completely lost the superstitious terror which surrounded their first equine contacts. The horse was completely integrated into the pattern of Indian life and had the tribes been suddenly deprived of their new riding stock it would have necessitated a complete readjustment.

The Spanish colonists of South America soon found themselves confronted with a complex of tribes which they labeled *Los Indios Caballeros* or "The Indian Horsemen." These tribes were the terror of the pampas, often raiding as far as a thousand miles in bodies of five and ten thousand warriors. But they were not essentially brave men, for we find many accounts in which their individual lack of courage is stressed, again and again. In 1822 John Murray wrote *An Account of the Abipones, an Equestrian People of Paraguay* and from it emerges a picture of these people. Their principal arm was the lance, which they had emphasized after the introduction of the horse. In battle they depended on a mass charge with lances leveled, to take their objective. The bow, which had been superseded by the lance, was made of one piece of wood and was as tall as a man. In cross section the bow was rounded and the principal wood used for its construction was the *neterge*. Bowstrings were made from plaited fox guts or from the braided fibers of certain palms. Around their camps they used a second type of bow for bird shooting. It was extremely short, never being over three feet in length, and with an extremely light pull. The flat string used with it was three inches wide, fashioned from liana bark or flattened bamboo. From this small bow the Abipones shot clay pellets, holding the fingers well across the string so that it remained flat at full draw. With any ordinary bow such a draw would be impossible, but the extremely light weight allowed the Abipon bird hunter to keep the pellet between his fingers, at the same time positioning the "string" so as to gain the maximum accuracy.

For war and hunting the longer bows were used, but the point which must remain clear is that the bows were made just as they had been before the coming of the horse. The bowyers made no concession to changing times, and for this reason, when the men wanted to shoot, they dismounted from their horses. Most of their arrows were made of reeds, with a hardwood head of the drop-off type. Crow feathers were used for fletching the various arrows, and the feathers were glued on with a mixture of vegetable gums and boiled fish bladders. To protect their arms the archers wore wooden arm guards, fashioned to follow the contours of the arm. Quivers were made of reeds, lashed around hoops of liana. Various types of arrowheads were used—for war and for different kinds of hunting. Before going into battle the warriors sorted out their best shafts and put them to one side of the quiver so as to have them readily available.

Most buildings in their territory were made of light, inflammable materials, and each war quiver carried its complement of kapok-headed arrows which were lit before shooting. When the fire arrows hit the palisades of a frontier town or tinder dry roofs, it became an easy matter for the archers outside to mount and ride in, unopposed. Yet for all their successes and their massive raids *Los Indios Caballeros* failed to produce battle tactics which would ultimately spell victory. They refused to modify their bows and depended on the shock contact of their lances against the fire power of matchlocks and the body armor of the white settlers. Even dismounted, their bows, which pulled an average of sixty pounds, were not able consistently to pierce armor, so that the Spaniards were comparatively safe. The greatest damage inflicted by the Indians was on poorer settlers and their own kinsman, who had become Christianized and lived in the Spanish towns and settlements.

In the United States, warfare on the plains was an entirely different matter. First we must remember that when the whites first came to this continent, all movement was through essentially wooded country lying along the eastern seaboard. Spanish infiltration in Florida and the southwest was primarily confined to gold hunting and the religious conversion of the Indians. The acquisition of land for purposes of agriculture and settlement was secondary. The active struggle by the tribes against agricultural invasion was almost entirely confined to the eastern settlements of the French, English and Dutch. Here the white colonists encountered tribes who fought with stealth, who used every subterfuge, specialists in the art of ambush. White learned from Indian and Indian learned from white. By the year 1709 the Indians of the Carolinas were stealing empty beer bottles from the settlements for use in making arrowheads. The extremely sharp cutting edge of glass was superior to their own stone heads and they readily accepted the "new" product, glass, into their thinking.

Woods warfare was almost always conducted at unbelievably short range and for this reason the effectiveness of the bow was greatly reduced. In his *History of the Troubles of New England* George Hubbard quotes an instance: "I seized hold of a firebrand, at which time an Indian drawing an arrow would have killed me, had not one Davis, my sergeant, rushed forward and cut the bowstring with his courtlace." While the bow is an excellent weapon for ambush because of its silence, it is not at all suited to hand-to-hand combat. Most of these early battles in the colonies were between individuals—tomahawk versus sword, musket and pistol against the bow. In those rare cases where regular troops were used against Indians, the soldiers suffered severely. No more striking example can be offered than Braddock's defeat during the French and Indian Wars.

In open country, fighting took on a completely different complexion. Here the quality of ambush was dependent on isolated geographical features, and the element of surprise became the most valuable weapon on either side. The Cheyenne, Sioux, Pawnee and Crow warriors were superb horsemen, but unused to and psychologically unequipped for pitched battle. Their bravery was unquestioned—more than one instance is recorded where individual warriors rode into hopeless situations in an almost medieval sense of chivalry and gallantry.

Their weapon, the bow, played a vital part in the whole pattern of their lives, occupying an almost religious position. They were composites made of sinew and wood or in some case of horn and sinew. They used the flat form of the bow which, while not as effective as the recurve, was at least better suited for mounted warfare than the longbow. They had used fire arrows against one another in tribal raids, and when the settlers trekked out onto the plains and prairies in canvas-covered wagons, the Indians found the flaming arrows were equally effective against these new enemies.

The white man, however, received at this point a technical aid which actually won the plains for him. The invention of a repeating rifle was the real turning point in the long series of Indian Wars. Previous to its use in the west the white man had been at a distinct disadvantage. Fighting in open country, without benefit of cover from which to fire, hide and reload, the rifleman suffered since the Indian could shoot a minimum of eight arrows to one gunshot. Few people have stopped to realize that if the repeating mechanism had not come along when it did, the advance of the white man across the plains would have been postponed indefinitely, if not entirely stopped. Faced with superior fire power in the hands of his enemies, however, the Indian rapidly lost the fight, and by such time as he too was equipped with repeating firearms the white conquests were too great to be retaken.

The North American plains tribes were quite capable of realizing their position and acting on it, as long as they had the advantage of heavier missile fire. Had they, like their South American counterparts, depended on the lance, the rapid-fire mechanism would not have been needed.

Some authorities are inclined to disagree with the premise that the South American Indian was the less adaptable. They say instead that the difference in the utilization of the horse in combination with primitive weapons came as a direct result of the difference in the fauna of the two continents. They point out that the buffalo was the root of the North American plains culture and that pursuit of that animal gave the northern tribes years of experience in developing techniques of mounted hunting, which were readily adaptable for warfare. In South America the buffalo did not exist, nor were there any comparable forms on which *Los Indios Caballeros* could practice and perfect such skills. Therefore, they say that the South American tribes were at a distinct disadvantage when the white invasion occurred, due to a flaw in faunal distribution. Then they point out that South America was the home of one tribe which with bow and spear held off Spanish attack so successfully that they were ultimately the victors, from a military standpoint, and that this cannot be said of any North American tribe. These southern fighters, the Araucanians, employed the normal Indian tactics of ambush and surprise but combined with them the elements of military organization and discipline, which finally won for them the grudging concession from the Spanish that the tribe was to retain uncontested possession of their tribal homelands in southern Chile. The final factor which gave the Araucanians a distinct advantage over the majority of the other tribes was a terrific tenacity of purpose which allowed them to suffer many defeats without at the same time losing purpose.

The question of accuracy among Amerindian archers is one which cannot be settled with any degree of ease. Referring again to Ishi, Pope's friend and mentor, we find that he was the usual superb woodsman and hunter, but even Pope did not feel Ishi would have become a great tournament archer. Again it must be stressed that the Indian used his bow as a means of livelihood, and his only interest lay in making every shot count. If the first arrow brought down the deer or the enemy it was sufficient, the archer was not seeking anything as abstract as a high score. Tallies of game taken or enemies killed were for the long winter nights in the form of recitative song, the essence of the moment was to cook and eat each target.

Certain tribes did gain a reputation as marksmen and it is hard at this date to say whether it is based on actual fact or rather on the surprised reactions of the chroniclers. Columbus encountered such a tribe on his first landfall at the island of Dominica. His sailors, putting ashore, were speedily repulsed by a shower of poisoned arrows and "The Admiral of the Ocean Sea" hastily pulled anchor and made for a neighboring, less hostile island.

Dominica, that first island, was one of the homes of the Carib Indians, and is in fact their last stronghold today. The Caribs were warlike, childlike and totally incapable of assimilating European culture. For many years anthropologists argued as to the original home of the tribe but finally, through linguistic likenesses, established the fact that their point of origin was in that mass of jungle and river which forms the headwaters of both the Amazon and the Orinoco. Moving down the latter at an early date, they debouched into the Caribbean, sweeping away the indigenous Arawaks by a combination of cannibalism and rape-marriage. When white civilization impinged on the Caribs, the invaders found themselves embroiled in a series of violent battles. The history of the Caribbean is full of stories of colonists versus Caribs and none is more colorful than this extract, published in 1608. It is from a book entitled *Another Class of Indian News: or a true and tragical Discourse, showing the lamentable Miseries endured by Sixty-Seven Englishmen.* In spite of the somewhat quaint wording used by the author, John Nicol, it is a vivid story and in many ways typical of a thousand battles—it could have been fought in New England or Brazil as easily as on a Caribbean island.

"Then came the arrows so thick out of the wood that we could not get our match in (here Nicol refers to the custom of applying a slow-match to the powder of a matchlock gun) for pulling them out of our bodies, so amongst our band there were but five or six pieces discharged, which, when the Indians saw give fire, did fall flat on the ground, shouting and crying with a most hellish noise, naming us they our names when their arrows pierced us.

"So when they saw we could not hit them with our pieces they would come so near us as though they purposed to make choice of what place to hit us. Some they shot in the faces, others through the shoulders and of others they would nail the feet and the ground together.

"Master Budge and Robert Shaw ran both into the sea and were drowned or killed with arrows. Master Finch had a little buckler [a light shield], with which he did save himself a long time but at last an arrow passed through both legs, what he could not go, and stopping to pull it out, they killed him;

and if any of us offered to run at one or two savages, straightway they fled a little distance, but suddenly twenty or thirty
would enclose us, and still shooting arrows into them until
they were down, with a great Brazil sword they beat them
to death. [The Brazil sword was a great two-handed weapon
of extremely hard wood, from which it took its name. In
South and Central America the sword was often serrated,
with obsidian-studded teeth.] Master Kettleby did behave
himself very gallantly, for he did not respect what arrows he
received in his body as long as he could reach one stroke at a
Caribbee; but they were too nimble for us, in regard they
were naked. Yet, nevertheless, we ran through them all, thinking if we could escape that ambush there had been no more
trouble to us; but as I was pulling arrows out of his body,
to the number of twenty at least, a third ambush burst out
of the woods, from whence came arrows and hit him in the
breast, which he perceived would be his death, for he could
not stand but I held him; and I was forced to let him go and
shift for myself.

"Then I overtook young St. John, his body almost full of
arrows, of which I pulled out a number; but what for the
blood that ran from him and the extreme heat he was in
from his flight, he failed to overtake the rest of our company
that was before.

"And still the Caribbees did gather ground upon us, and
arrows came thick about us on every side.

"And then the poor youth willed me to entreat his men
to stay; and so having overtaken one, I caused him to stay,
which he was not willing to do; for he told me his sword
would not come forth of the scabbard, so I took hold of the
hilt, and betwixt us both pulled it out; but before we made
an end, these cruel and bloody Caribbees had encompassed
young St. John; yet to my grief I did stand and behold his
end, who, before he fell, did make them give back like so
many curs before a lion, for which way soever he ran they
all fled before him. His body was so loaded with arrows that

he fell to the ground; and upon one hand and knee did he keep them from him with his sword, so much he scorned basely to die at their hands.

"Myself and the man whose sword I had helped to set free were not the only marks they aimed at; for having rifled young St. John's body, they pursued very hotly, which caused us to make haste to four of our fellows who were entered into a narrow path leading through the woods from the sands, to the houses where we dwelt. But there was in that path another ambush, which drove us back to the sands; and when they saw us so hardly chased they entered the path with us again.

"On one side thereof there was a high mountain; the other went down to a low valley. The first four of our friends took up the mountain, by which means they offered too fair a mark for them to hit, who dropped them down, one after another.

"All this time, neither Harry, Peter Stokesley's man (a merchant now in Bucklersbury) nor myself was shot; but as we thought desperately to burst through them into the narrow path, there came an arrow and pierced quite through his head, of which he fell suddenly, and I ran to lift him up, but he was dead without speaking one word to me at all.

"Then came there two arrows and hit me in the back, the one directly against my heart, the other through my shoulder blade; so sword in hand I ran upon them desperately, thinking before I had died to have been the death of some of them; and in my running I saw Captain Anthony [the colonists often gave Christian names to the Indians as well as honorary awards of title, usually in keeping with the individual's tribal standing] with an arrow in his bow drawn against me, who stood until I came very near him, for he purposed to have sped me with that shot, which when I espied it coming, I thought to have put it by with my sword, but, lighting upon my hand, it passed through the handle of my weapon, and nailed both together. Nevertheless, I con-

tinued running at him still and before he could nock another, made him and all the rest turn their backs and flee
into the sands again; which opportunity when I espied I
leaped into the wood, down to the valley, where I found a
salt lake; and hearing them with loud shouts and cries, which
they use in times of triumph and victory, pursue me still, I
leaped into the water, with my sword nailed to my hand and
two arrows in my back, and by the help of God swam over,
but with much ado, for the further side was shallow and I
waded in mud up to the waist, which had almost spent me."

The Caribs were trained in archery from infancy, like
many primitive races who use the bow. The men of the
tribe prided themselves on their ability as drinkers, seamen
and warriors. Permanent settlements were built of bamboo,
palm or woven reeds and the men ceremonially bathed each
morning and then allowed themselves to be stained bright
red from head to toe by the women. The rest of the day was
devoted to hunting, the making of bows or arrows and
drinking. War was a spontaneous thing, rising often from
alcohol rather than from any insult to the tribe—but when
white invaders threatened, the whole nation sallied forth
in defense of their islands.

In the cradle the male children were subjected to head
deformation. Flat slabs of wood or stone were bound against
the front of the forehead so that when the child was able to
walk, his forehead slanted backward from his brows. The
Caribs believed that the process thickened the frontal bones
of the skull, so that as an active warrior the Carib was not
afraid to receive blows full on his head. Strangely enough,
there are many instances in the history of the islands where
these men took blows from steel blades on these deformed
areas without any apparent ill-effects. If this was a result of
the deformation we cannot wonder at its prevalence, but an
interesting sidelight is thrown on the matter by the writings
of the Reverend Thomas Davies, who in 1606 said that he
had been reliably informed by the Caribs themselves that

the purpose of the binding, and the subsequent bone growth, was to permit the men to shoot straight up into a tree from its foot. Seemingly forcing the frontal bones backward enabled an archer to shoot with accuracy directly overhead and in rare cases even further. Davies also says that the Caribs consistently hit a coin the size of a half dollar at a distance of 225 feet, while children, using a toy bow made of a bent stick, could hit a small clay target twenty times in succession at thirty-six feet.

A little over a century after Davies, the French Dominican, Jean Baptiste Labat wrote enthusiastically of the Caribs' archery abilities. He described their attacks on settlements when from the shelter of big trees they set fire to the houses. Then, still concealed in the bush, they picked off their opponents one by one as they fled from the burning buildings. He says that the children were given bows and arrows to use as soon as they were weaned, and that at the age of ten they never missed a mark from a distance of fifty yards. For their elders, Labat reserved the greatest admiration, for they would shoot birds from the trees when the good father could not even see the targets. As bona fide sea people, they used the bow and arrow to shoot the fish which thronged the waters around the islands, attaching long fiber strings to each arrow, at the end of which was a float to mark the position of the victim. Their bows were made of several woods and were all strung with specially selected lianas. Arrows were made of long, straight reeds, but the heads, of the drop-off type, were of fire-hardened, notched hardwood. For use in war, the arrowheads were dipped in the juice of the manchineel tree, a deadly vegetable poison. Labat says that they fired their arrows so rapidly, particularly at birds, that many observers were of the opinion that more than one shaft was nocked at a time.

The rapid and accurate arrow fire of the Caribs and their successful use of arrows against the whites is only one of hundreds of instances where Amerindians obtained some degree of victory over the invaders. Again and again, the Spanish found to their dismay that the best Toledo steel was but little safeguard in their campaigns against the natives. One South American tribe, the Tomoyo, earned a fearsome reputation with their arrows, one Spaniard recording that "an arrow sent by one of them would fasten the shield to the arm that held it; and sometimes it has passed through the body and continued on its way with such force as to pierce a tree and hang quivering in the trunk." During the fighting in Florida the troops suffered so many losses due to their armor being pierced that they were convinced for a time that they were dealing with witchcraft. Accustomed to stopping ball with their breastplates, the soldiers could not understand how Indian arrows, made of slender reed and tipped with hardwood, could penetrate with such ease.

Of the three hundred horses which accompanied the expedition when it landed in Florida, 270 were killed by Indian arrows. The Creeks, Choctaws and Chickasaws opposed to the Spaniards were quick to realize that the Spanish, afoot, were easy targets and concentrated their fire on the animals. The Spanish saved the last few horses after an experiment proved to them once and for all the effectiveness of the arrow.

An Indian captive was offered his freedom if he would show his captors how arrows were made to pierce steel. Accordingly, the heaviest coat of mail in the camp was selected and hung over a heavy woven basket. The Indian, from a distance of 150 paces or three hundred-odd feet, promptly strung his bow and drove an arrow completely through the target from front to back so that the arrow fell on the ground behind. Then the soldiers put a second suit of armor over the first and again the Indian shot. This time, the arrow did not completely pass through the mark, but came halfway out through the back. Spanish tactics, following this demonstration, were abruptly revised and their body armor was almost completely abandoned. They padded their few remaining horses with several thicknesses of felt, to a depth of

four inches, which was much more effective in stopping the
deadly shafts. The men themselves wore body armor composed of alternating layers of felt and rawhide, but even
this was not arrowproof for in one instance an arrow penetrated steel plate, an inch of felt, a layer of cowhide and
continued into the horse for nine inches.

Armor piercing by Indian arrows was by no means confined to Florida and South America. Our own Southwest
produced good archers, quite capable of driving their shafts
through Toledo plate, and the practice continued among
the desert tribes for many years. In 1794, in Cologne, a Jesuit
priest published an account of his years in the Mexican state
of Sonora. In it, Father Pfefferhorn speaks of the remarkable
power of Indian arrows, but before going into his own words,
there is a moment's digression on bow strength. Pfefferhorn's
account speaks of the Apache Indians and that tribe certainly
raided into what is now Sonora. But in a series of bow tests
conducted by Dr. Saxton Pope, to which we have previously
referred, it was found that the bow of the Apache—or at
least those specimens tested by him—was extremely light,
with an average pull of twenty-eight pounds. On the other
hand Sonora was and is the home of another tribe called
the Yaqui. These sturdy mountaineers proved a thorn in the
side of the Mexican government for many years until, under
Porfirio Diaz, troops forced a mass removal of the Yaqui to
Yucatan. Today the remainder of the tribe are peaceful
agriculturists, at least on the surface, but complete masters
of their own territory. Pope also tested Yaqui bows and
found that they had an average pull of seventy pounds, a
draw weight far more suited to fit in with Father Pfefferhorn's
story. We can either believe that the Apache bows degen-
erated in just over a century, or we can make a substitution
and read "Yaqui" for Apache in the following quotation:

"The Apaches are incomparable archers and their arrows
seldom miss. Their arrows when let fly by a strong arm have
more power and effectiveness than a bullet from the best

musket. As a proof I cite only one example, to which I myself was witness. A mounted soldier was dispatched by his
captain with letters to the captain of another garrison. His
cloak tightly folded up lengthwise lay below him on the
saddle and fell partway over his left leg. Covering the cloak
and the same leg hung his shield, made of three-ply, very
thick oxhide, used for protection against arrows. Beneath
the saddle was a thick cover of oxhide which hung down a
little over the horse's belly. The soldier rode past a mountain
where some Apaches lay in ambush and was struck by one of
their arrows, which passed through the shield, through the
many folds of the folded cloak, through the leg of the soldier,
finally through the leather cover and penetrated almost a
quarter of an ell deep into the body of the horse. A bullet
would scarcely have such force. When the soldier arrived at
the place where I then was, I myself saw with amazement
what had happened."

From the foregoing accounts, it must not be supposed that
Indian arrows were invincible. All too often they blunted
themselves on the armor of the white men, glancing harm-
lessly off. But even then the Amerindian learned. If his arrows
were not effective against one part of the body, he aimed for
those parts which he knew were vulnerable. Thus at the
Battle of Mauvila, eighty-two Spaniards were besieged by
several groups of Indians, and among the Spanish casualties,
eighteen were shot either in the eye or the mouth, where
body armor and helmets proved no protection. And in another battle between the Spanish and Indians, this time in
South America, one conquistador was struck in the head and
shoulders by fifty-three arrows.

Although all Amerindian archery had a common root, if
we accept the theory of Asiatic origin, there was, as we have
said, a tremendous amount of variation in the equipment
used when the white men first established contact. Sioux
bows were only four feet long in some cases and at the other
extreme the Tauapuery, on the Rio Negro in Brazil, used

bows which were nine feet, ten and a half inches long. The Costa Rican Indians used no feathers on their arrows, while the Iroquois and the tribes of Tierra del Fuego used a two-feather fletch, which rifled around the shaft in a fantastic pattern. Some tribes sewed the feathers on, others glued them on and a few, following the Eskimo custom, forced the feathers into the wood. Fire arrows were common on both continents, as were arrowheads especially adapted to bird hunting. Among the Xingu in Amazonia the warriors went into battle naked, but the tribes along the northwestern coast of Canada, copying their Siberian ancestors, wore armor made of reeds when they fought, using composite bows. The Mandans used shafts cut from a variety of small trees, well feathered and headed but with no nocks, while in South America many tribes used a midshaft of reed, with both a drop-off head and nock.

Fletching among the Amerindian tribes represented the apex of their decorativeness, insofar as tackle was concerned. Perhaps a few more centuries of uninterrupted development would have resulted in more highly stylized equipment, with emphasis on ritually inspired pattern and decoration. Such might well have become the case with the Aztecs, if in the course of culture they had developed the practice of burying arms with their dead. They believed that a soul going to heaven, must venture through a purgatory peopled with monsters and hellish abominations. To protect itself the soul carried a bow and a quiver of arrows. If, then, the Aztecs buried after-life equipment, as did the Mongols, we might have seen some beautiful archery tackle but unfortunately decoration of bows, arrows, quivers and arm guards was either a matter of personal taste or tribal identification. A single glimpse of an arrow on any frontier, north or south, is usually more than sufficient for the old-timer to identify the archer.

The Indians themselves gave any number of accounts for the origin of archery. One common version was that a grateful god or demigod made a gift of the knowledge to his people. Another fairly common legend was the old, world-wide idea that the inspiration for the bow had come from the porcupine and his quills. The Baccairi, one of the Xingu complex, attributed archery to the semi-diving hero Keri, who also created the various peoples of the world out of the different reeds which were used for arrows. These same Xingu often planted large crops of reeds, called *uba* to insure that at any given time the tribe would have a plentiful supply of arrow shafts.

In our own Northeast there is a quaint and charming legend about the origins of archery which has about it the ring of authenticity. The tale is of a warrior out hunting bear with a spear. Suddenly the hunter finds himself face to face with a large female bear in the midst of very thick undergrowth. Finding that discretion is the better part of valor, the hunter turns and starts to run away from the enraged animal. Tripping, he falls flat on his face and lies there, expecting every second to feel the grip of the bear and her hot breath as she closes in for the kill. Finally after what seems an age, he turns to see that the beast is lying dead on the ground behind him. In the haste of his flight he caught the butt of his spear against an overhanging vine, which, acting like a bowstring, propelled the spear into the closely following bear. The now victorious warrior returns to camp with the idea for a new weapon, plus the dead bear.

On the plains the gift of archery came from the Buffalo God, who decreed that his people should use this weapon to clothe, feed and house themselves, from the fruits of the hunt. Prior to the introduction of the horse, the plains tribes had hunted on foot, depending on the tremendous annual migration of the buffalo herds to provide them with meat. This dependence on migration was duplicated farther north where both Indians and Eskimos used the movements of the caribou to provide them for the entire year. In the north the animals were driven through traps to bring them within bowshot, while on the plains the Indians used camouflage or sometimes drove the herds over a cliff to insure the annual supply.

The horse, however, changed the picture entirely, bringing the hunter into constant contact with his quarry. The tribes followed the game, so that there was seldom a period of dearth. Galloping alongside his quarry, the mounted hunter drew back his arrow and drove it into the forequarter of the buffalo. Most of the tribes, including the Pawnee and Cheyenne, used bows with enough power to completely pierce a buffalo so shot. Even when an arrow did not completely penetrate the animal, the rider continued alongside, knowing that the rocking gallop of his prey would soon work the now imbedded arrow into some vital part of its anatomy, thereby finishing the kill. Most of the bows on the northern plains were made of ash, well backed with sinew, especially among the Crow and Sioux. Farther south the bows were made of osage orange, again backed with sinew. Buffalo furnished the sinew in both cases and it was first softened by long boiling, then laid on in strands, parallel to the long axis of the bow. These long fibers were fastened to the bow with cross-lashings of more sinew, tightly knotted to prevent slip. Sometimes the cross-lashing assumed the form of a pattern which ran the length of the bow, thereby assuring a better grip for the long strands. But in most instances the bindings were four in number, with two above and two below the handle. Occasionally the long sinews were softened by chewing rather than boiling, but this was work done by the women.

The quivers worn either in war or on the hunt were of buffalo hide, with the fur turned in to protect the shafts. The outside of the quiver was ornamented with gay beadwork and porcupine quills, dyed with bright vegetable colors. The Sioux used two types of arrows, for hunting and for war, although in actual practice the two were interchangeable. The war arrow featured the head set so that it lay parallel to the bowstring, while in many cases the hunting shafts were set so that the head formed a right angle with the string. The heads themselves were about three inches long in the case of the hunting arrows and from four and a half to five and a half inches long for the war types. Catlin, the early writer and artist, noted that most of the plains tribes held the bow on the diagonal, and other chroniclers say that the mounted bowmen had a tendency to hold the bow almost on the horizontal in many shots.

Many of the arrowheads were grooved and most authorities have assumed that the grooves were for the purpose of letting the blood run freely. However, since there was such a degree of penetration, there was seldom a case where "bloodletting" would be necessary, and any bow hunter will tell you that wounded game will bleed quite freely with the ordinary pattern of arrowhead. Moreover, the Indian did not customarily bleed his kill, preferring it with the blood in. A more valid explanation is that the groovings were instead a primitive and stylized representation of lightning. So engraved, the arrow took on a magic quality, supposedly capable of killing as quickly as the thunderbolt.

The bow and its accouterments played such an all-important role in the plains life that even after the warriors and their families were driven onto the reservations and the buffalo had all but ceased to exist, the hunters clung to archery. When the government ration of beef was issued to them on the hoof, the men rode up alongside, as they had with the buffalo, and shot the cows and steers down with well-placed arrows.

It was only natural that in such a bow-dependent society, the arm should take on certain sociological tones which were well removed from the field of the hunt. In 1866 the Sioux tribes met in solemn council with the Northern Cheyenne, their traditional enemies. Both were strong, warlike races but the Cheyenne had, in part, accepted the white men. The Sioux were still violently opposed to white occupation of tribal lands, and they had called the Cheyenne to discuss war against the whites and their fortification of the Bozeman Road. The war chief, Red Cloud, proposed to lead both nations in an all-out fight against any further encroachment.

The Cheyenne decided against coöperation and announced in council that they would continue to side with the whites. Then the Sioux heaped upon them what was considered to be the final insult. Each Sioux member of the council took his bow from its place and proceeded to beat his Cheyenne opposite number with the weapon. Such a flogging, with an unstrung bow, was traditionally reserved for dogs, and eloquently expressed the Sioux's feelings.

Unfortunately many of the records and accounts of the South American tribes remain locked in their Spanish and Portuguese original forms. We know that generally the tribes in those areas followed a pattern of fighting and war similar to the tribes of the Caribbean and our own eastern seaboard. Ambush and surprise were their supreme weapons and they placed their dependency on close-range shots.

Hugo Meyer, the German, maintained that in all his experience the only South American bows encountered were self, never composite. Also, they were almost universally large, averaging more than six feet in length. The only exceptions which he found were those which occurred in the Guianas, the llano country of what is now Venezuela, the Gran Chaco and Tierra del Fuego. The Guiana bows were the smallest of the lot and tended to bear out the theory postulated by Friedrich Ratzel, who did much research on the subject of archery in Africa. Ratzel says that bows used in forests are smaller than those used in open country, because the forest, by restricting freedom of movement, forbids the use of large bows.

It is difficult to see how Ratzel could have come to this conclusion. It may hold true in Africa but certainly is not true in regard to either North or South America, nor is it true of Asia, where we have seen the shortest bows of history in use in open country. In open lands—savannahs, pampas, steppes, llanos—the success of the archer depends on maximum effective cast, and where the hunt is on foot, on the hunter's ability to conceal himself and his weapons. A longbow, in order to achieve the same cast which is inherent in a recurve, must perforce be almost unmanageable due to its extreme length. Nor would such a bow lend itself to ready concealment if the hunter were stalking in open country.

Whereas in forest country the hunter used every available means to get as close as possible to his target before he shot, he had the advantage of natural cover. Nature assisted his stalk and his choice of weapons was not so restricted. He might have used a shorter bow, with an increased cast, as easily as he did the longer bow. That he did not is because the shorter, stronger bows—flat bows, recurves, composites— with their extreme casts are derivative from the forest bow and not the reverse. One will come closer to reality, if instead of accepting Ratzel's theorem as is, it is interpolated to say that the bow used in forests is generally weaker, since the nature of the terrain restricts movement and forces dependence on stealth, woodscraft and even poison. On the other hand the bow in open country may be longer only in the sense of possessing a longer cast.

Because the South American bows were wood, and usually of one piece, they were often reinforced, for at least part of their length, with windings of fine bark or fiber. The bindings were dyed and the pattern in which they were woven formed tribal identifications. Sometimes, too, small bunches of feathers would be added to the binding pattern to further distinguish the craftsmanship of the maker.

In cross section the bows were nearly circular, becoming thinner toward either end and flattening out into the form of an ellipse. Nocks at either end were rather crude, the wood being cut away a little to form a shoulder where the string could rest. Strings were made of many substances, fox guts, as in the case of the Abipones, *tocon* with other tribes and often with twisted palm fiber of one sort or another. The bowstring was tied by a knot at one nock and ran to the other end, in the strung position. At the loose end, the string was wound around the limb of the bow several times, working toward the handle. As the string became thinner, due to its taper, it was finally twisted about the bow and tied off on itself.

Bows were for the most part in a simple arc, although in some cases bowstaves were chosen with a natural dip at the handle, which gave them the form of a double curve. The true reflex has been found but rarely, the examples being exceptional and usually made from natural wood growth, rather than by a process of shaping and forming. Some of the bows are made with a grooved back so that the hunter carried one arrow on the string and a second held against the bow, thereby eliminating the necessity for a quiver.

Unlike the North American Indians, who used bracers made of furs and hides, the South American tribes often dispensed with the bracer entirely. It is there, however, that the most ornate bracers occur, among certain Brazilian Indians who made the arm guards from contrasting macaw feathers, laid with their quills toward the archer's wrist. After the introduction of the horse, plaited horsehair was sometimes used for arm protection.

In retrospect Amerindian archery seems to lag far behind the heights achieved by the bowmen of England and the horse archers of Asia. Even a man who knew Indians and archery as well as Will Thompson, said that "good shooting by the North American Indian was rare." There are, however, two sets of circumstances which must be taken into consideration before Indian archery is dismissed so lightly.

When Thompson made his statement, the Indian was on the decline and had been for many years. Subjected to white influences, contaminated by our culture and its artifacts, the Indian had lost faith in his own inheritance and was as yet unable to absorb completely what we offered as a substitute.

No individual, or race, caught in such a dilemma would be capable of high-caliber performance with the tools of the older, no longer, acceptable culture. To assess the ability of the Indian as an archer at such a point is unfair and, moreover, unreliable. We cannot easily forget the Florida brave piercing the test armor for his captors nor the conquistador with fifty-three arrows in his head and shoulders.

Secondly, with few exceptions, the Indian had not reached a particularly high level of achievement. He used the bow through necessity and for that reason he used it effectively. Had he not done so he would have ceased to exist. Like any race of hunters, in any part of the world, at any time in history, the Indians used the bow to perform satisfactorily the tasks which enabled him to survive. The Indian was a hunter first and a warrior secondly. The power-dominated Aztec and Inca cultures are the exceptions to the rule. Essentially the Indian became a warrior to protect his hunting grounds or to extend them if their yield was not sufficient for tribal needs. His primary concern with the bow, then, was as an instrument to supply him with food. The Indian may have many critics as an archer—but few question him as a hunter.

The modern field archer and his brother the bow hunter owe the Amerindian a tremendous debt. Without carefully studying and applying the Indian field practices, it is doubtful that any man will kill much game with a bow. The Indian may never have set a world's record for distance, or scored six "golds" in a tournament, yet his skills—of tracking, of stalking, of moving through the open like a ghost, are indispensable to any man who hunts with a bow. Every year, as more and more of us turn to hunting archery, our debt to the red archers increases.

9

Just Yesterday—and Tomorrow

IT IS ENTIRELY PROBABLE THAT THERE ARE MORE ACTIVE
archers in the world today than at any other period in history.
And while most of today's bowmen do not practice through
necessity, the fact does not in the least change the terrifically
high standards of shooting which are in evidence every day.
Certainly, from a standpoint of equipment available, the
modern bowman is head and shoulders above any of his predecessors.

So far as we can judge from recorded history, there has
never been a total lapse in archery since its inception. It has
been called "the sport of man since time began," and if its
present popularity will serve as any indication, it will continue for many more thousands of years. As long as there are
any undeveloped areas with primitive people, the bow will
play an active part in their everyday lives. In civilized areas,
with their growing emphasis on sports and relaxation, it is
entirely probable that archery will continue to enjoy an ever-
increasing popularity—for the sport has a universality of appeal which is unequaled. At a recent national competition
held in England the oldest shooter was over ninety years of
age, and most of us are aware of the ease and natural aptitude
with which children approach the bow.

Modern archery in the United States is directly derivative
from two sources—the European and the Amerindian. "Cow-
boys-and-Indians" has, with us, developed all the qualifica-

tions of a folk game and our first crude bows are usually patterned after Indian models. Yet the strength of archery today would never have developed without some sort of formalization, such as existed in England during the early years of this country and which, in fact, still continues in a large degree. The Amerindian influence is particularly strong in field archery and bow hunting—which form a terrifically large segment in the whole of today's archery picture.

Many archers are unaware of just how long the sport has existed on an organized basis in the United States. The year 1828 saw the first target archery in the country. Perhaps, earlier, in colonial times, the sport had been practiced, but if so we have no knowledge of it and the credit belongs to the young men who founded the Club of the United Bowmen of Philadelphia on September 3, 1828. Dr. Robert Elmer, in his classic work *Target Archery*, has given us a wonderfully complete picture of that early shooting in the City of Brotherly Love. Suffice to say that the members were inspired, not by Indians, but by England and they ordered their first tackle from there. They first shot the York Round in 1844 and by that date were well enough organized to have a distinctive club shooting uniform—"white duck trews, iron-gray jackets with black braid trim and peaked caps of bombazine." The Club of the United Bowmen of Philadelphia is still active, and to it all American archers owe an eternal debt, not only for first formalizing and organizing the sport, but also far having kept it alive through many years of ups and downs.

As a sport, archery grew slowly. The nation was itself expanding, fighting wars, suffering growing pains, and people had neither the time nor the inclination to devote much time to any sport or recreation. Shortly after the years of the Civil War, enough people had become interested to allow a national tournament to be held. In 1879 the United States witnessed its first really big shoot, held in Chicago at the White Sox Baseball Stadium.

The choice of these grounds necessitated a change in shooting practice, and as a result, our style of shooting is different today from that used by archers in most countries abroad. In tournaments, arrows are shot in groups known as "ends." In England and in the United States, prior to this first national, it had always been the practice to place the targets at either end of the field and shoot three arrows at one set and, after picking them up, to shoot three more in the reverse direction, the six arrows constituting an "end." At Chicago a new version of the end was introduced and has since taken its place in all American shooting. This is an end in which all the targets are at one side of the field and at which all six arrows are shot. The organizers of the tournament felt that for the archers to shoot back on the second half of the end, toward the spectators, was too dangerous and therefore ordered the change.

The task of first really popularizing archery fell to two brothers, Maurice and Will H. Thompson. Born in the South shortly before the Civil War, the Thompsons found at the end of hostilities that they were practically landless persons and they took to the woods. Out of this period of semi-hermitage they developed a tremendous skill in archery and woodscraft, which was brought to the attention of the general public through a series of magazine articles and books, most of them written by Maurice, the older of the brothers. Even today the works are vastly readable, showing an almost poetic flair for description. The main effect, however, was to awaken in the American consciousness a strong interest in archery, the out-of-doors and "a return to the simple skills of our forefathers." The Thompsons provided the impetus which kept archery alive during a period when only a few scattered clubs were actively engaged in shooting.

The second wave of public interest in the sport occurred just after the First World War. Then Dr. Saxton Pope and his hunting partner, Arthur Young, proved conclusively to the general public that archery was a vital sport, full of excitement and thrills. Many a youngster today, drawing his bow, imagines that he is sighting for one of the magnificent African lions which formed part of their formidable bag. Both Pope and Young are, unfortunately, now dead but their place in putting archery before the public has been ably taken by Howard Hill.

To say that modern archery owes its overwhelming growth to Hill is to risk instant censure from archers, not only in this country but all over the world. Immediately it will be pointed out that the late Dr. Robert Elmer brought to archery a devotion seldom exceeded, that the late Harold ("Uncle Hat") Titcomb promoted archery unceasingly on both sides of the Atlantic—so much so that he became the only American elected president of England's Royal Toxophilite Society. Such comments are perfectly true and it is also true that men like Paul Klopsteg, Forest Nagler, William Folberth and Fred Bear—to name but a few, have done truly amazing things in every phase of archery—theoretical and practical. To acknowledge Hill's pre-eminence in publicizing archery today is by no means meant as a detraction, nor does it ignore the contributions past, present and future of other stalwarts in the field. It is simply that Hill, mainly through the medium of the motion picture, has familiarized more people with the excitement, beauty and enchantment of archery, than any other single archer. Roger Ascham is properly the "Father of Archery," but one needs to be an archer really to understand and appreciate his work. To see Hill at work is to gain an interest in archery today, and more importantly, it often fathers the desire to imitate and to participate. It is this initial process of familiarization which ultimately adds to the constantly growing number of archery addicts. If the other archery greats were as well known to the general public it would be a different matter. As it is, Hill through his own films, his writing and his excellence as a technical adviser, has brought archery into millions of places where it would be otherwise unknown.

After World War II, archery began to grow so rapidly in

the United States that psychologists became interested in the reasons behind the sudden acceleration. The results of their research are far from conclusive, but in the main they feel that due to emotional and psychological pressures created by present-day living and by international tensions, there is a growing tendency to find older and perhaps more primitive methods of relaxation. They point out that there is a direct correlation between the increased interest in archery and the current spurt in camping. One writer, N. N. Hostages, has even gone so far as to say:

"In this return to archery, we may be seeing a subconscious desire for survival preparedness. The inner man may be thinking that if all else fails, if civilization ceases to exist in today's terms, I may as well be prepared to defend myself— in terms which are basic and sufficient, no matter how low the level surrounding me." In support of Hostages' hypothesis, nine young Frenchmen in 1956 isolated themselves in the mountains in an attempt to prove their own survival abilities. Their weapons were the bow and arrow. Although the causes may still be obscure, archery remains the fastest growing sport in the United States today.

Archers in this country are extremely fortunate, in that there is enough space for them to shoot. Bold though that statement may sound, one has only to look at English and Continental archery to realize its truth. We are so used to space and room that we find it hard to imagine that today in England there is not one single field archery course, for nowhere on the island is there the prerequisite amount of land which can be used exclusively for the sport. In direct contrast, according to a recent report in the New York *Times,* there are within a radius of forty miles of Times Square 125 archery clubs, most of which either own or have access to a standard field course.

Archery as we know it is broken into two main classifications, each with its own governing body. The older of the groups, administered by the National Archery Association, concerns itself with target and tournament shooting. The second group comes under the National Field Archery Association, which deals with field shooting and its correlative, bow hunting. The NFAA is a comparative newcomer in the field, having been organized in 1939, whereas the NAA dates back to the first big tournament in Chicago in 1879. The two associations represent organized archery in this country, although there are actually millions of archers who shoot without any form of affiliation.

Figures for the total number of archers in the United States today vary considerably. The *New Yorker* magazine has stated that there are eight million archers, while the New York *Times* puts the figure at two million. A recent survey by a sporting goods association estimated seven and one half million and other groups consider ten million to be accurate.

Of the total, the most active section is that of the field archers. "Field archery" as the term is used today, is a modernized and formalized version of an older archery game called "roving." In roving a group of bowmen would move through open country picking targets as they progressed. Usually the archer who succeded in hitting the chosen target could elect the target to follow, and the game proceeded as long as the players were willing. Naturally such practice, because of varying distances, different terrain, changing winds and odd elevations, brought the archer into top form for hunting. It taught him to use his instinctive ability to such an extent that it became reliable, and adapted to any situation. Field archery came from these roots and is today the first and best training ground for the bow hunter.

We can get some idea of the influence played by field archery and hunting by a comparison of figures between the United States and England. If we accept the figure of seven and one half million archers in the United States, it means that out of our total population, one person in every twenty-five is an archer. In England, where we must remember that archery is almost exclusively confined to target shooting, there are approximately fifteen thousand archers, which means that there is one archer out of nearly thirty-four hundred inhabitants. We cannot blame this lack of interest entirely on a lack of field work and hunting, however, because today the cost of archery equipment in England places the sport beyond the means of many who might otherwise become converts.

With the spread of civilization and its not unmixed blessings there has been a consequent decrease in the number of primitive archers. The bow and arrow is no match for the rifle and the motorcar, so that only isolation preserves those few remaining cultures which cling to the bow as a way of life. In certain sections of Africa the natives, who were once skilled archers, wait for white hunters to provide them with their occasional gorgings of meat—civilization has apparently robbed them of the initiative to carry on with their own old patterns. There are no laws which keep them from killing their own meat in the traditional way—it is simpler to wait for someone to kill for them.

Modern repeating rifles are too much for the bow in open warfare, even when the latter is backed by indomitable courage. The tumult of our own wars against the Indians had scarcely died when across the globe another race made a last-stand battle with bows. In 1896, the Moslem Amir of Afghanistan, Abd-er-Rahman Khan decided to convert certain of his subjects to the law of Allah. His troops, complete with rifles and mountain guns, marched into the mountains and valleys of the Hindu Kush to effect the conversion. The Kafirs, whose ancestors had fought against Alexander in these same valleys, held out against the Moslems as long as they could, using longbows and a few flintlock rifles. In the end, modern fire power won. Islam and rapid fire produced a hard-fought and bloody victory over arrows and animism. The occasional Kafir huntsman still uses the bow—but he prays to Mecca five times a day. The story of the Indians in the United States, the story of the Kafirs in the Hindu Kush are not isolated instances; they are typical of what has gone on and is going on, all over the world. This is "an age of progress" and progress means change. The bow and arrow as a way of life are doomed through this same change, which leaves no room for cultures as wasteful and backward as those which cling to a hunting pattern.

Because of this, any search for bow-using people is confined to the backwaters of today's globe. Not too long ago the world was shocked by the death of a group of missionaries in northern South America. Seeking to convert the Auca Indians, the men met death by arrows and the formidable poisoned darts of this tribe. Such cases become rarer every year. In some sections of the far North the poorer Eskimos still use the bow, but only if they cannot afford the luxury of a rifle or a shotgun. There, as in many other areas, the use of the bow is dictated by economic necessity rather than any desire to cling to the older ways. No doubt this is equally true of the tribes in northern Siberia, about which we know so very little. We do know that the march of collectivism has spelled the end of tribal ways throughout much, if not all, of Central Asia. The ends of Communism are not served by the free ways of archer horsemen. Refugees fleeing from mid-Asia bring word that the nomadic archers are fast disappearing, and any indication of unrest among the tribes will no doubt come to the same inevitable conclusions which overtook the Kafirs in the Hindu Kush.

South of the Himalayas, in the immense area which was called the China-Burma-India Theater during World War II, remote hill tribes still use the bow and poisoned arrows against game and the occasional intruder, but they form isolated pockets in their war against progress. In the hill states such as Bhutan and Sikkim, archers form part of the standing army. Fortunately for them, they have not yet been mustered against modern, mechanized armies. Farther south still, in the Andaman Islands, the few remaining natives are as skillful with the bow as were their ancestors. Asia today, far from being the home of the world's finest bowmen, is a continent where archery is an anachronistic survival, marking time against the inevitable day when progress—materialistic and political—will consign it to the scrap-heap of colorful yesterdays.

Japan alone represents an area where archery has successfully survived the transitional stages. Militaristic tradition, based on the Samurai, has allowed Japan to keep archery in an honored place. As with so many Japanese customs, archery is ritualistic to a high degree. The bows are differently proportioned from any other form known today. All the bows with which we are familiar are constructed so that the handle approximately bisects the bow length, whereas in the Japanese bow, the handle is well down on the lower limb. When the bow is drawn, the arc of the upper limb is considerably longer than that of the lower and the upper limb must be made proportionately weaker. The bow arm, too, must be positioned so as to compensate for this difference and the Japanese shoot with the bow arm high, their anchor point falling above the ear. The bows themselves are almost always made of bamboo, and archery is taught with what amounts to religious solemnity. It is, as we have said, linked with the teaching of Zen Buddhism, so that every movement, every action of the archer becomes part of a pattern designed to teach him some metaphysical truth.

The Japanese, having achieved "modernity," have saved archery as a part of their cultural heritage. And perhaps it is not too much to hope that in times to come, other Asiatic nations may return to the sport. In our haste to grasp at progress and advancement, we are often inclined to forget or negate the benefits which may accrue from holding on to some of the old ways.

The question of African archery is so completely involved with that continent's sudden "coming of age" that it presents rather special problems. We have largely ignored African archery up to this point for the simple reason that few

African tribes of consequence depended on the bow in any great degree. In common with hunters all over the globe, the natives used the bow, but their utilization was largely predictable, based on necessity and with little to mark it from any other primitive bow-using culture. One thinks primarily of Africa as the land of the spear, and although the bow was and is widespread on the Dark Continent, it is not the weapon most commonly associated with the African warrior. Within the past ten years one native rebellion against colonial forces involved the use of the bow, but this does not alter the fact that the warlike races—Zulu, Masai, Ashanti— have been spearmen.

Africa is responsible for one of the most colorful arrowheads in the world. Called the ogee, the head eliminates the need for feathering on the shaft, but its use is restricted to certain specific areas. The head is in the form of a modified S curve, which during flight has the effect of spinning the shaft. Since this is the function of the feathering on an arrow, the ogee does not require fletching. Remarkable though this innovation may seem, the resultant arrow will not fly quite as true as a fletched shaft and the ogee cannot be said to represent a great archery advance. It is instead a departure, which proved not altogether successful.

We have dealt at some length with the Bushmen of South Africa in a previous chapter. One phase of archery among these Stone Age survivors deserves special mention, however, for it is here that "Cupid's bow" becomes a reality.

Most of the few remaining pure Bushmen are confined to the interior of the Kalahari Desert, an immense semiarid tract of land. Here, cut off from the rest of the world, the Bushmen live as their ancestors lived, thousands of years before the white men and thousands of years before the Bantu invasion from the north. Their courtship begins when a young man of the tribe feels attracted to one of the girls. At night, sitting around the communal fire, he watches her, covertly, hoping that she will respond. If in the course of time she seems to reciprocate his feelings, the man sets about making a lover's bow. Cut from the horn of an antelope, it is perhaps the only self-horn bow in the world, a tiny thing, less than a foot in length and with a draw measurable in ounces. The accompanying arrows are slender, unfletched, self-pointed bits of wood, cut from the thorn trees, which grow in profusion all through the Bushman territory. All these preparations are made in deepest secrecy and are ignored by the other members of the tribe.

When at last the bow and its arrows are finished, the young man follows the girl of his choice out into the bush, where she is engaged in gathering nuts or fruit. From a safe place of concealment, reached after a long and careful stalk, he shoots a shaft at the girl and watches tensely for her reactions. If she keeps the little arrow, it is a sign that she has agreed to become his mate. If, on the other hand, she throws the tiny shaft away, she indicates to him that his love is not returned. The end of the courtship, if it has been successful, comes when he places a specially prepared cloak of hides about her shoulders in front of the rest of the tribe. By using the bow, he avoids public humiliation, should the girl have her eye on another man.

Bushman music too, is inextricably mixed with the bow. It is the only instance today where the double use of the bow continues as it did millenniums ago. At night the men sit about the fire with strung bows at their sides. One of them will pick the bow up, and with his hand pressing the string against the handle, insert one end of the bow in his mouth. The taut string forms a striking surface and the mouth and cheeks serve as a sounding box. As the string is struck or plucked, the resulting high whine is amplified around the circle of listeners. These bow tones form the basis for all Bushman music.

South and Central America furnish their share of primitive bowmen, even at this late date. Much of the interior of South America is truly *terra incognita,* so much so that the few explorers moving through it come out with tales of "white Indians," giant lizards and buried cities. But we need not look to find anything surprising about archery when these areas are finally fully explored. The bows may be more highly decorated, the arrow poisons more effective, but in general they will conform to the patterns we have already examined in South America.

In southern Mexico and northern Guatemala the Lacadones, descendants of the Mayas, still make lovely longbows, fashioning them from a variety of tropical woods. But these are a shy and peaceful people, seeking only solitude, and their arrows are reserved for the deer which flees through the jungle or for *el tigre* as he stalks their flocks. In Baja California the Seris, surely the most decadent of tribes, make pitiful, flimsy bows, with thin reed arrows. Not so long ago they tipped the arrows with unpleasant poisons, but today they are so exhausted and so near extinction that even the art of making arrow poisons has been lost among them.

Most of today's archers, then, are located in the United States. Here, in a land which prides itself on progress, this oldest of sports is making an astonishing and steady comeback. Every year more schools, colleges and universities teach archery. Every year more and more hunters join the ranks of bowmen who seek their prey with deadly shafts. Archery has a universality of appeal which places it high on any list of participant sports. It is not a sport which will ever appeal to mass audiences, since to watch archers shooting can be boring, at best. Yet there is something so instinctive about archery that if a child is given a bow and arrow, the reaction is far swifter, far smoother, far more accurate than that which follows the similar gift of a gun.

Conservationists have welcomed archery with open arms. To them the return to bow hunting offers at least a partial solution to the problem of ever-decreasing resources. With a steady rise in population and a steady decrease in open lands suitable for hunting, it is growing harder and harder to accommodate the thousands who annually feel the call to hunt. The bow hunter by the nature of his equipment is forced to rely more on skill and woods ability than the man with the gun. In a given season, from a percentage standpoint, far fewer deer are killed by archers than by gun hunters. Moreover, before an archer is skilled enough to hunt with any degree of success, he learns to look before he shoots, to act with more caution—with the direct result that any given acreage can support more archers than gunners.

One must not suppose that archers suffer psychologically because they kill less game. Quite the contrary—most bow hunters get as much excitement from a clean miss as a gunner derives from a clean kill. The atavistic impulses awakened when we take bow in hand are often reward enough in themselves. To seek an analogy we must look to fishing, where the way a well-dressed fly lands on the water is as important to the purist as the catch itself. Bow hunting, to be successful, forces the practitioner to become so absorbed in his stalk that he loses all sense of self.

The inability of the average city man with gun in hand to differentiate between a white-tailed deer and a Jersey cow has led more and more farmers to post their land. Each year we find it necessary to drive farther and farther from the urban centers in order to find land open for hunting. Nor can the landowners be blamed—their livestock, their property, often their own lives are jeopardized by the outrages of trigger-happy, licensed gun toters, who at other times of the year are ordinary peaceful citizens. To the farmers, the archer seems a blessing, for the bowman sees what he shoots at and has long since learned to tell a dog from a fox and a boar from a bear.

Most states today have legalized bow hunting and in the majority of cases have established regular bow seasons for the benefit of archers. In certain special cases and areas, bow hunting is the only legal method of taking game, the land otherwise being closed to all hunting. And there have been rumors to the effect that one state will close all its land to gun hunting, allowing only archery, until such time as its stock of wild life has reached a more equitable balance.

Sportsmanship in the hunt is a necessary thing and not simply fair play to the other men in the field. It also means that the hunter gives the game an equal chance. Everyone who goes out to hunt knows, or should know, one basic rule of sportsmanship—never leave wounded game. Unfortunately in today's body of hunters there are many—too lazy, too ignorant, too wantonly cruel—who do not even attempt to track down animals they have wounded. Game wardens in every state will tell you of case after case of gun-shot game left to die and rot, of hopeless cripples left to starve. In these instances it is seldom the archer who is the culprit, for those same age-old impulses which turn men into archers will compel them to follow to the end, no matter how bitter and tiring the trail. In saying this we do not mean that all gun hunters are poor sportsmen, or that all archers are paragons of virtue. Instead let us say that an animal wounded by your arrow becomes a magnet, a personal challenge, which cannot be ignored.

A few years ago pictures were published in eastern newspapers of deer found dead of arrow wounds, out of season. An immediate hue and cry was raised by unfriendly interests, attempting to put an end to bow hunting. The gist of the outcry was that archers were sadistic poachers and lawbreakers, totally lacking in sportsmanship. Naturally, no mention was made of the number of deer found annually which are killed out of season with rifles and shotguns.

Closer examination, however, proved that the deer were victims of organized poachers, using crossbows. Both the longbow and the crossbow lend themselves to silent killing but it is the latter which best lends itself to the purposes of market hunters.

Had this case not been investigated, archery would certainly have suffered at least lost prestige, if not lost privilege.

Conservation authorities were willing to check the matter thoroughly because they knew from experience the law-abiding, sportsmanlike attitude of bow hunters in general. Among any given number of individuals there will inevitably be a certain percentage of lawbreakers. There were poachers among the bowmen of Merrie England, but to date, fortunately, archery has not appealed to a large number of commercial-minded killers, nor to the so-called sportsman whose sole motivating principle is the biggest number of trophies. If the number of bow hunters ever equals the total of gun hunters, such an estimate of ethics may well have to be revised, but currently it is true.

Archery equipment has kept pace with the number of archers. Never before in history has tackle been of such a high caliber. New methods and materials are constantly tested and tried to give the bowman all the benefits of modern science. Now we have steel bows, aluminum bows, glass bows and plastic bows, and it will not be long before we have magnesium bows. Our arrows today are matched to within such a degree of tolerance that only a trained technician can differentiate between them. Design has reached the stage where any bow you buy is the child not only of centuries of experience, but also of high-level theoretical engineering. Every material—natural and synthetic—which can possibly be used in archery has been tested and experimented with —with varying degrees of success. We can rest assured that as man advances from a technical standpoint, archery will adopt for itself any changes, any innovations which will be beneficial.

From our vantage point the future of archery seems bright. The same psychological forces which have motivated the recent interest in the sport seem likely to continue and we can reasonably expect to see the total number of archers increase with every passing year. And certain factors tend to make us think that with the passage of time archery will become even more popular.

Although many of us either ignore or are unaware of the fact, we are rapidly using up many resources of the globe. It is entirely possible to calculate with nicety the number of years left during which we may enjoy unlimited coal, oil, steel and a dozen other materials which we now take for granted. The shortages which will follow may not, in all probability, occur during our lifetimes. But they will happen and when they do, people will of necessity have to resort to simpler, less than-expensive sports and relaxation. Bows have been made of wood before and they will be made of wood again—and there will be trees on the earth, long after the last coal has been mined and the last iron ore has been dug. Our grandchildren may find that archery is their forte for the simple reason that guns are beyond the means of the private citizen or because the ball bearings essential for roller skates are only allocated on a high priority. Certainly such speculations are purely hypothetical, but they do not lie in the realm of total impossibility. One need only say that continued, uncontrolled depletion of planetary resources will make it necessary for all mankind ultimately to revert to a simpler pattern of existence. An existence which will, in all probability, involve the use of the bow, not as a weapon—but as an arm of enjoyment.

There is, of course, another alternative—the world of space ships, pressure domes and interplanetary mining. Spectroscopic examination has long shown us that the moon is rich, and who is to say when the first ships will land there and then voyage farther. A few years ago such ideas were confined to Jules Verne and the wilder comic books; today they are soberly regarded as "near possibles" by many scientists the world over. And sober archers, who might decry science fiction, have debated solemnly about the possibilities of shooting on the moon. There, a shot from a flight bow might, with only partial earth gravity, travel over two miles, or might it?

When our ancestors first stepped out of the cave, they

carried their bows. Down through the ages which have inter-
vened, man has never let go his hold of this, his first powerful weapon. Like the dog, it has served him well—in war
and in peace. It has defended his home and guarded his
flocks; with its help he has built great nations and with its
aid he has reduced tall cities. When those first men penetrated into the next valley, which was to them another world,
they carried their bows. When and if our descendants set out
into space to other worlds, it is not too much to suppose that
they will carry bows—if only as a means of relaxation?

INDEX

222   *Index*